Ron Fry's

How
To
Study

Ron Fry's

How
To
Study

Revised Edition

THE CAREER PRESS
180 Fifth Ave.
PO Box 34
Hawthorne, NJ 07507
1-800-CAREER-1
201-427-0229 (outside U.S.)
FAX: 201-427-2037

HOW TO STUDY
Revised Edition
ISBN 0-934829-93-4, $8.95

Cover design by Dean Johnson Design, Inc.

Excerpt on p. 20 reprinted from **The Perfect Portfolio** copyright © 1991 by Marilyn Seguin and used with permission of publisher, The Career Press.

Copies of this volume may be ordered by mail or phone directly from the publisher. To order by mail, please include price as noted above, $2.50 handling per order, and $1.00 for each book ordered. Send to: The Career Press, Inc., 180 Fifth Ave., P.O. Box 34, Hawthorne, N.J. 07507

Or call Toll-free 1-800-CAREER-1 (in Canada: 201-427-0229) to order using your VISA or MasterCard or for further information on all books published or distributed by The Career Press.

Table of Contents

How To Study

HOW TO
Use
This
Book

What one knows is, in youth, of little moment;
they know enough who know how to learn.

— Henry Adams

How to *study?* What's the big deal? You're no brain,
but you've got a "C" average. Besides, you don't have *time*
to do more—football practice starts Monday.

And why would you want to waste your time reading a
book about something you're not particularly crazy about
doing in the first place?

Believe it or not, there are some terrific answers to
those questions. But before I start convincing you why developing proper study skills really *is* important, let's

figure out exactly what we mean by "study skills" so we're all on the same wavelength.

Yes, *How To Study* includes hints, advice and techniques for taking notes in class, while you're reading your textbooks, even in the library. And how to prepare for tests. And how to organize your study schedule to get the best results in the shortest amount of time. But that's the *last* half of the book. There are essential skills you may think don't even have anything to do with studying and important steps you need to take right from the start.

OK, where do I start?

> Learn as though you would never bo able to master it; hold it as if you would be in fear of losing it.
> — Confucius

Developing great study habits is like a race between you and all your friends around a track. Before you can declare a winner, you have to agree on where the finish line is. In other words, how do you measure your ability to use these skills? What's good? What's poor?

But you can't even start the race until you know where the *starting* line is—especially if everybody is starting from a different place on the track!

Chapter 1 starts by explaining each study skill and clarifying how each can and should function in your life. Then you have the chance to find your own starting line.

This first chapter is the most important in *How To Study*, because your own honest assessment of how well you have already mastered basic study habits will set the tone for your entire approach to the guidelines you will find throughout this book.

In Chapter 2, you'll learn the importance of where, how and when you study and start building the study environment that's perfectly right for *you*. Why is this important? If you've spent three hours reading **Moby Dick** with Poison shaking the walls, it's not surprising that you're still on shore. Reading and understanding Mr. Melville might have little to do with increasing your reading comprehension, rescheduling your time or changing books...and a lot more to do with just turning down the volume. (Alternatively, those of you who have trouble studying in a hush-hush library might find a Walkman actually helps you concentrate!)

There is no magic elixir in the study habit regimen. If math and science are not your strong suits, scanning **How To Study** will not transform you into a Nobel Prize-winning physicist. Nobody is great at *every*thing, but everybody is great at *some*thing. So you'll also get a chance to rate the subjects you like and dislike, plus those classes you do best and worst in. You'll find in later chapters that applying yourself to the subjects in which you need the most work is a simple, logical and successful way to alter your current habits without necessarily studying harder or longer.

Chapter 2 also introduces some of the "intangibles" in the study equation: your home environment, attitude, motivation, etc. If you are dedicated to the study discipline and motivated to achieve certain goals, all the other factors that affect your study habits will fall more naturally into place. A belief in the study ethic is one of the keys to success.

Reading and comprehension

Chapter 3 introduces the skills basic to any study process: reading and comprehension. No matter how well you learn to take notes, how familiar you become with your library, how doggedly you study for tests, if you are reading poorly (or not enough) and not understanding what you read, life will be difficult.

Becoming a good reader is a skill, one usually acquired early in life. If it's a skill you haven't acquired yet, now is the time!

Effective reading is a combination of comprehension and retention. Chapter 3 will help you find the proper balance of these elements. It will also help you work on concentration—the ability to focus on the printed page to the exclusion of all else, a skill all superior readers have.

Learning how to remember more of what you read is more important than reading faster. Chapter 3 also points out how your ability to recall ideas, facts and figures can be significantly increased (both quantitatively and qualitatively) with the right kind of practice.

"If I only had more time!"

To see a significant change in your life, many of you will not need to study *more,* just *smarter*. Which means making better use of your study time. Chapter 4 introduces organizational and time management tools you can use to make sure you are always on track, including guidelines to develop both short-term and long-term calendars.

Go to the head of the class

In chapter 5, I talk about the one experience we all have in common, no matter how old we are—the classroom. I'll help you take better notes, encourage your active participation in class discussions—including pointers on how to overcome the more natural tendency to hide behind the potted plant in the back of the room—and get more out of lectures.

Learning your library

Chapter 6 introduces you to the single most important resource in your study career—your library. Whether you live in a small town, where library volumes are counted in the thousands and "current" might mean five years old, or a large city, where the library stacks kiss the sky and contain answers you don't even have questions for yet, learning how to take advantage of this great collection of knowledge is very important.

You'll learn about the kinds of books, periodicals, newspapers, magazines, computer software, video and audio tapes and other reference materials available to you and suggestions for how to find and use them, including an explanation of the Dewey Decimal Classification System.

Move over Mr. Dickens

No matter how confident you are in your writing ability, I doubt you cheer when papers are assigned. Get used to it. In college, term papers are a regular part of virtually every class you take. And don't think graduation ends the chore. You'll be writing "papers" of some kind—business letters, presentations, proposals, long memos—in almost any career you choose. And your ability to clearly and concisely express your views and communicate facts, figures and ideas will strongly influence how fast you advance in your chosen career.

I'm convinced that too many of you place the emphasis in "writing papers" on the word "writing." In Chapter 7, I'll introduce you to a remarkably easy way to gather research, take notes and organize your information. By breaking down any paper, no matter how complex, into easy-to-follow steps, I think you'll find you create papers infinitely better than before—even if you're still no threat to Mr. Dickens when it comes to writing.

Use a no. 2 pencil

Chapter 8 covers the do's and don'ts of test preparation, including the differences between studying for weekly quizzes, midterms and final examinations, why last-minute cramming doesn't work, studying for and taking different types of tests (multiple choice, essay, etc.), how to increase your guessing scores, even which questions to answer first and which to leave for last.

That's nice. So what?

Now that you know what you're going to learn from this book, why bother going through the whole thing?

Well, the answer sounds like one of those "Why?" "Because!" scenes your parents put you through: Whether you *want* to, whether you *like* to, you do *have* to study. For better grades? To get into a better college? Succeed in school? Keep your parents off your back?

In part, but not really: *Learn to study to succeed in life.* Sooner or later, you'll be out of school. But you will never *not* have to study—you might as well get the habit early.

Whether you want to be an engineer, doctor, construction worker, artist, dancer, auto mechanic or businessman, be prepared to study. Never have the demands of our society been so great and the burdens on individuals so weighty.

What you know *now* and can do *now* is all anyone else cares about. It may come as a surprise, but once you get your first job, hardly anyone will ever again care about where you went to high school, attended college, the clubs you were in, the sports you lettered in, even—shock of all shocks—what your grades were. Day-to-day performance will be the major criterion for keeping your job, getting raises and earning promotions.

Even if we discount the intangible benefits of education—a more complete and fulfilling life, access to more and more interesting people, places and things, etc.—the practical rewards of education can be measured in very real dollars and cents terms: The more you learn, the more you earn.

No senior citizen discounts

> A man must always study, but he must not always go to school.
>
> — Montaigne

You will always have to study. Don't believe that when you finally leave school—whether as a dropout or with a Ph.D.—that your days in the classroom and library are over. You will encounter new classrooms throughout your lifetime.

Land any but the most menial job and chances are there will be a training program. The more complicated the job—whether it's primarily manual or professional—the faster and more often you will find yourself back in the classroom. Some training programs at major corporations last for months.

Yes, you'll be back in school, whatever your age, and it's too late to learn how to study now!

Taking notes? Watch what happens during that first sales meeting when 40 new products are flashed on the screen, one right after the other. You'd better be ready to quickly and accurately write down what you need to know to go out and explain them to your prospective customers.

Asking your boss to repeat himself again and again doesn't wash in the real world.

Job promotion? Even if your lack of advanced schooling forced you to start at a clerical or blue collar job, your natural talents might send you up the ladder of success. When that promotion to a white-collar job or even a management position does come, you'll be happy to know your company is paying all your expenses for that highly touted, three-day management training seminar. Yes, it's intense.

Yes, you'd better be ready to learn and assimilate the material quickly. And yes, you're back in school again!

The list is endless—birth training sessions, art classes, the entire range of adult education classes, languages, dance, sculpture—whatever interests you, whatever you want or must learn, will require developed study skills. Through all stages of life, opportunities to acquire new knowledge and expand your horizons will constantly present themselves. Will you be ready to take advantage of all those wonderful opportunities?

Master the fundamental study habits, and you'll shout "yes!"

How smart do *you* study?

Will this book really help you? Yes, it really will. *How To Study* is the most comprehensive study guide ever written—a fundamental, step-by-step approach that *you* can follow to develop and sharpen your study skills.

If you're struggling through college or graduate school, here's your life raft.

If you're a high school student planning to attend college, hone your study skills *now*.

If you're heading for trade school, planning to dance, write, paint, etc., not considering college, even if you're ready to drop out of high school at the earliest possible instant, you need *How To Study*.

And if you're an adult returning to the classroom after a lengthy absence, there is no substitute for the rules you will learn in this helpful collection of study procedures.

If I only had a "C"

What if you're a really poor student?

So what?

How smart you are is not the point. *What counts is how smart you study.*

With the possible exception of those 2 percent of you who qualify as "gifted," the effective study habits *How To Study* teaches will help students of any age:

If your grades are average to good, you will see a definite difference.

If you are on the borderline of the pass/fail range, you will benefit considerably.

If good study habits are in place but rusty as a result of years away from the classroom, *How To Study* is the perfect refresher for you.

And if you *are* one of those "2 percent gifted," I *still* think you'll find some helpful techniques in these pages.

Does it work?

The answer is a resounding "yes!" One obvious example is the performance of Asian immigrant students in American schools. Hampered by an unfamiliar language, they have nevertheless almost unanimously demonstrated superior academic achievement.

Is it genetic? Something to do with rice? Humidity? Monsoons?

No. Studies indicate these students simply excel at incorporating the study ethic—a combination of strong motivation, discipline and a solid adherence to time management—into their everyday lives. And like muscles that are regularly exercised, study skills get stronger and better with practice.

That's what's ahead in *How To Study*. Learning, practicing, honing and strengthening the many skills we'll be discussing in the following pages is no small task. Some will be easier to master than others, yet each plays a definite role in shaping your study habit armament. They are all interrelated, all interdependent, and all must be mastered if the whole is to work effectively. It's a task I'm certain you can accomplish.

This new, revised edition of *How To Study* incorporates the feedback I've received from parents, teachers and, most important of all, students since the book was originally published in 1989. I've included additional topics and expanded on others. And I've referred you to the other valuable books in my brand-new **HOW TO STUDY** *Program* for more detailed information on taking notes, writing papers, managing your time and improving your reading.

Before you continue reading *How To Study*, take a day or so off to let the impact of what you can learn—and what it can mean in your life—sink in. Then turn to Chapter 1 and complete your self-evaluation. I think you'll find you already know far more than you think you do!

Chapter 1

HOW TO
Start
Out
Right

It is not enough to understand what we ought to be, unless we understand what we are; and we do not understand what we are, unless we know what we ought to be.
— T. S. Eliot

Taking a good, honest look at yourself is not the easiest thing in the world to do. In the next two chapters, I'm going to help you evaluate the current level of all your study skills—a necessary step to identify the areas in which you need to concentrate your efforts—identify the study environment and learning style that suit you; and categorize all of your school subjects according to how well you *like* them and how well you *do* in them.

How to keep score

In the next few pages, I'm going to explain the 10 primary study skill areas covered in this book: reading and comprehension, memory development, time management, library skills, textbook note taking, classroom note taking, taking notes in the library, classroom participation, writing papers and test preparation. Then I'm going to ask you to rate yourself on your current level of achievement and understanding of these important skills: "A" for mastery or near mastery of a particular skill; "B" for some mastery; "C" for for little or none.

Remember: There are no right or wrong answers in this assessment—no pass/fail determination. It's only a place to start, a jumping-off point from which you can measure your progress and rate those areas in which your skills need improvement.

In order to simplify the process, I've listed the primary study skills on page 19. Take a separate piece of paper and rate yourself on each of the 10 skills (from reading to test preparation) *before you read the rest of this chapter.* After you've rated yourself in each area, give yourself two points for every A, one point for every B, zero points for every C. If your overall rating is 15 or more, excellent (give yourself an A); 10 to 14, good (give yourself a B); and if nine or less, fair (give yourself a C). Mark this rating under Initial Study Skills Evaluation.

Now, let's review each of these areas, giving you insight as to what "fair," "good" and "excellent" really mean. As you read each section, go ahead and fill in your rating on the chart on page 19—and be honest with yourself. This evaluation will give you a benchmark from which to measure your improvement after you have completed the book. File it away and make the comparison when you've completed reading.

Your Starting Point

Initial Study Skills Evaluation	A ( )	B ( )	C ( )
Reading	A ( )	B ( )	C ( )
Memory Development	A ( )	B ( )	C ( )
Time Management	A ( )	B ( )	C ( )
Textbook Note Taking	A ( )	B ( )	C ( )
Classroom Note Taking	A ( )	B ( )	C ( )
Classroom Participation	A ( )	B ( )	C ( )
Basic Library Skills	A ( )	B ( )	C ( )
Library Note Taking	A ( )	B ( )	C ( )
Writing Papers	A ( )	B ( )	C ( )
Test Preparation	A ( )	B ( )	C ( )
Overall Study Skill Level	A ( )	B ( )	C ( )

Reading

Speed, comprehension and recall are the three important components of reading. Comprehension and recall are especially interrelated—better to sacrifice some speed to increase these two factors. To test your reading and comprehension skills, read the passage on page 20, close the book and jot down the one, two or more key points made in the selection you read, then review the text and compare your notes with the reading selection. You will get a good idea of how well you understood what you read and just how good your top-of-the-mind recall is.

Some journalists begin their writing careers by "stringing" for a newspaper. A stringer is a reporter who covers the news in a specific city or region for a newspaper located in another city. The stringer writes the story or, more often, calls in the information to another writer on the newspaper staff. If this type of freelance writing interests you, contact the managing editors of several metropolitan newspapers for more information on opportunities. Keep in mind that the assignments you will get as a stringer will probably be routine "cover-the-meeting-in-200-words-or-less" stories; the meatier assignments are saved for staff writers.

One of the best ways for a writer to get published is to freelance an article for a magazine. Although it is difficult for a novice to get published in many of the high-paying national publications (there are exceptions, so keep trying anyway), there are hundreds of smaller publications that rely on freelance contributions for much of their editorial content. These publications pay anywhere from several cents per word to several hundred dollars for a completed article.

To break into magazine freelancing, you need to follow these five steps: Generate an article idea, find potential markets (magazines that might accept an article on your topic), do preliminary research on your topic, query the editors of the magazines, and, finally, write the article.

Score:

If you can read the material straight through and accurately summarize what you've read, all in less than two minutes, give yourself an A. If you have some problems reading and understanding the text but are able to complete the assignment in less than five minutes, give yourself a B. If you are unable to complete the assignment in that time, remember what you read or produce accurate notes at all, give yourself a C.

Retention

There are specific methods to help you recall when you must remember a lot of specific facts. One of these is memorization—committing information to word-for-word recall. Memorize only when you are required to remember something for a relatively short time.

When memorization is required, you should do whatever is necessary to impress the exact information on your mind. Repetition is probably the most effective method. The key, it has been determined, is to repeat the memory sequence of study, then recall. Language students, for example, have been taught to string together sentences in what soon becomes a short story or dialogue. Each day, new words are added and the student is required to remember and "parrot" them back the succeeding day. This add-on process has the effect of both stretching the memory (to make its capacity larger) and exercising it (to make the recall mechanism work more effectively).

Test #1: Look at the number following this paragraph for ten seconds. Then cover the page and write down as much of it as you can remember:

187654334357395860

Test #2: Below are twelve "nonsense" words from a language I just made up and their "definitions." Study the list for 60 seconds in an attempt to remember each word, how it's spelled and its definition:

Cernum	Thigh	**Numnum**	Chew
Erdur	Read	**Daved**	Man
Grendel	Book	**Armer**	Head
Batow	Run	**Hamich**	Elbow
Plitz	Think	**Frecum**	Jacket
Jotto	Kitchen	**Screb**	Twist

Done? Close the book and write down each of the 12 words and its definition. They do not need to be in the order in which they were listed.

Score:

Test # 1: If you remembered 12 or more digits in the correct order, give yourself an A; 8 to 12, a B; 7 or less, a C. Test # 2: If you accurately listed eight or more words and definitions (and that includes spelling my new words correctly), give yourself an A. If you listed from five to seven words and their definitions or correctly listed and spelled more than eight words but mixed up their definitions, give yourself a B. If you were unable to remember at least four words and their definitions, give yourself a C.

Time management

Your effective use of available study time can be measured by two yardsticks: (1) your ability to break down assignments into component parts (e.g., reading, note taking, outlining, writing); and (2) your ability to complete each task in an efficient manner. The following questions will help you assess how well you are allocating your time, how organized you really are:

A. How many assignments have you failed to complete in the last month because you forgot when they were due, lacked required materials when you needed them or got to the library too late to read the assigned books?

B. Do you have a weekly or monthly calendar?

C. Do you always carry it with you?

D. How much time do you devote to study per week?

E. How many "all-nighters" (or near-all-nighters) did you pull in the last month?

Score:

A. Give yourself one point for every such assignment; subtract five points if your answer is none.

B. *Add* five points for a "no" answer; *subtract* five points for a "yes."

C. *Add* two points for a "no"; *subtract* two for a "yes."

D. *Add* five points if you don't know; two points for less than four hours if in high school, less than 10 hours if in college; zero points for less than 10 hours in high school, less than 20 hours in college. *Subtract* one point for scheduled time greater than 10 hours in high school, 20 hours in college; five points if you study that hard but are convinced anyone else would have to study twice as long to accomplish what you do in half the time.

E. *Add* one point for each all-nighter or near-all-nighter. *Subtract* one point if "none." *Subtract* five points if your answer is "none" *and* you're an A or B student.

Use the chart below to see how you rate and how to grade yourself on this particular skill:

Test Score	Rating	Skill Score
-22 to -5	Excellent	A
- 4 to 0	Very good	A
1 - 5	Good	B
6 - 10	Fair	B
11 and up	Poor	C

Library skills

Using the library is a function of understanding its organization—and *using* it!. The more time you spend in the library—studying, reading, researching—the more productive you will be. You'll become adept at tracking down reference materials and finding the information you need quickly.

Virtually all libraries follow the same organization—once you understand it, you'll be "library literate," no matter which library you use. In this book, you'll discover what kinds of resources are available (books, periodicals, directories, encyclopedias, dictionaries, magazines, newspapers, documents, microfilm files), you'll learn how to select and find books (learning the Dewey Decimal System) and you'll find out about the functions of the library staff.

To better evaluate your library skills, answer the following questions:

A. What collections are restricted in your library?
B. Where would you find a biography of Herbert Hoover in your local library?
C. Where is the reference section in your local library?
D. Given the Dewey number for a book, could you find it in less than five minutes?
E. How often have you been to the library in the past six months? The past month?

Score:

If the answers to these questions are all obvious to you, indicating a steady pattern of library use, then you can claim to have the library habit—give yourself an A. If you can't answer one or more of the questions or will freely own up to a spotty record of library use, give yourself a B. If you don't have the faintest clue of where the closest library is, you get a C.

Note taking

Three different arenas—at home with your textbooks, the classroom, the library—require different methods of note taking.

From your textbooks: Working from your books at home, you should identify the main ideas, rephrasing information in your own words, as well as capturing the details you were unfamiliar with. Take brief, concise notes in a separate notebook as you read. You should write down questions and answers to ensure your mastery of the material, starring those questions to which you *don't* have answers so you can ask them in class.

In class: Class *preparation* is the key to class *participation*. By reading material to be covered before you come to class, you will be able to concentrate and absorb the teacher's interpretations and points. Using a topical, short sentence approach or your own shorthand or symbols, take notes on those items that will trigger thematic comprehension of the subject matter. Your notes should be sequential, following the teacher's lecture pattern. When class is completed, review your notes at the first opportunity. Fill in the blanks and your own thoughts.

In the library: What's the difference between taking notes at the library or working at home with library books vs. your own textbooks? Sooner or later you'll have to return library books (if you're allowed to take them out at all), and librarians tend to frown on highlighting them. So you need an effective system for library note-taking. In Chapter 7, I'll show you mine.

Score:

If you feel that your note taking skills are sufficient to summarize necessary data from your textbooks, capture the key points from classroom lectures and discussions and allow you to prepare detailed outlines and write good papers, give yourself an A. If you feel any one of these three areas is deficient, give yourself a B. If notes are what you pass to your friends in class, give yourself a C.

Participating in class

I don't know too many teachers who don't take each student's class participation into account when giving grades, no matter how many spot quizzes they pull, how many term papers they assign. And, you may have discovered, there are teachers out there who will mark down students who "ace" every paper and quiz if they seem to disappear in the classroom.

Score:

If you are always prepared for class—which means, at the very least, reading all assigned material, preparing assigned homework and projects and turning them in when due—actively participate in discussions and ask frequent and pertinent questions as a way of both trumpeting what you already know and filling in the gaps in that knowledge, give yourself an A. If you fail in any of these criteria, give yourself a B. If you aren't sure where the classroom is, give yourself a C.

Writing papers

Preparing any sort of report, written or oral, is 90 percent perspiration (research) and 10 percent inspiration (writing). In other words, the ability to write a good paper is more dependent on your mastery of the other skills we've already discussed than your mastery of *writing*. If you are an avid reader, familiar with your local library, a good note taker and capable of breaking down the most complex topic into the manageable steps necessary to write a paper, you probably turn in superior papers.

Score:

If you have already given yourself an "A" in Library Skills, Library Note Taking, Time Management and

Reading, give yourself an A. If you feel you turn in relatively good papers but definitely lack in any of these areas, give yourself a B. If your idea of writing a paper is photocopying the pertinent "Cliff Notes" and recopying the summary in your own handwriting, give yourself a C.

Test preparation

The key to proper test preparation is an accurate assessment of what material will be covered and what form the test will take. Weekly class quizzes usually cover the most recent material. Midterm and final examinations cover a much broader area—usually all the subject matter to date. Multiple-choice tests, essays, lists of math problems, science lab tests all require different preparation and applying different test-taking skills. Knowing the kind of test you're facing will make your preparation much easier.

So will creating your own list of questions you think your teacher will most likely ask. Through periodic review of your text and class notes, the areas in which your teacher appears most interested—and on which he or she is most likely to test you—should begin to stand out. As a final trick, prepare a list of 10 or more questions *you* would ask if the roles were reversed and *you* were the teacher.

Score:

If you are able to construct tests that are harder than the ones your teacher gives you—and you perform well on those—give yourself an A.

If you feel you know the material, but somehow don't perform as well as you think you should come test time, give yourself a B.

If you didn't pass your driver's test, let alone algebra, give yourself a C.

Your overall score

Once again, after you've rated yourself in each area, give yourself two points for every A, one point for every B, zero points for every C. If your overall rating is 15 or more, excellent (give yourself an A); 10 to 14, good (give yourself a B); and if nine or less, fair (give yourself a C). Put your new score in the section "Overall Study Skills Level" in the chart on page 19.

Now what?

The fact that you have been honest with yourself in evaluating those talents you bring into the study game is a big plus in your favor. Knowing where you are strong and where you need to improve makes everything else a good deal easier. Now, based on your test results, draw up a list of your assets and liabilities—your areas of strength and weakness. This will focus your attention on those areas that will require the most work to improve. As an example, a typical assessment might look something like this:

Study Skills Balance Sheet

Good	Fair
Time management	Memory development
Library skills	Class participation
Note taking	Reading
Test preparation	Writing papers

Interpreting your results

Assuming for the moment that this is *your* study skills balance sheet, what can we learn from it? Apparently you are relatively organized, familiar with and comfortable using the library, and get a good deal out of classroom lectures, your reading and library research. And you test well—or, at least, prepare well. So some key skills are already in place.

On the other hand, you don't read as much as you should and have trouble comprehending and remembering what you do. Your classroom note-taking ability seems to have been developed at the cost of full participation. And your ability to take notes and use the library has yet to result into good papers.

Congratulations! While I would strongly recommend you read the entire book, this simple test has enabled you to identify the chapters you really need to work on—in this case, 3, 5 & 7—and the specific skills that may require work long after you finish reading this book.

Once you identify which study skills you need to develop, you can then take your efforts one step further. After you finish reading **How To Study**, continue to read any of the other four books in my **HOW TO STUDY** *Program* that apply to your needs: *Write Papers, Take Notes, Improve Your Reading* and *Manage Your Time.*

Chapter 2

HOW TO
Organize Your Studying

My friend Mary is just entering her sophomore year of high school. She is bright, though she's never managed better than a B- average. Her school attendance record is spotty (at best) and she'd rather spend study time listening to music, shopping or just hanging out.

But reality is definitely beginning to snarl in the corner. The tiniest speck of motivation is just beginning to energize her study habits. She has sensed the link between study achievement and jobs, and she has recognized she will have to earn those things she wants. And that the money she earns is intimately connected to her grades.

The revelation has not transformed her into a scholar. Studying will always be a means to an end for Mary. She'll never like it, but at least she's recognized its utility.

Intrinsic and extrinsic motivation

Motivators are either intrinsic or extrinsic. What's the difference? You sign up for a voice class. While the hours certainly apply to your graduating requirements, you attend class because you love singing.

You also signed up for Biology. You hate the thought of dissecting frogs, and you couldn't care less whether humans are exoskeletons, endoskeletons or hydroskeletons, but the class is required.

In the first scenario, you are motivated by *intrinsic* factors—you are taking the voice class for no other reason than you truly enjoy it.

The second scenario is an example of *extrinsic* motivation. While you have no interest in biology, your reward for taking the class is external—you will be able to graduate.

Extrinsic motivation can help you make it through the boring or unpleasant tasks that are part of the process of reaching your goals. A vivid, visual image of your final goal can be a powerful motivating force. For example, one student thought about what his job as a computer programmer would be like whenever he needed a little help getting through difficult classes.

Try imagining what a day in *your* life will be like 5 or 10 years down the road. If you haven't the faintest clue, no *wonder* you're having a hard time motivating yourself to work toward that career as a final goal!

The goal pyramid

One way to easily visualize all your goals—and their relation to each other—is to construct what I call a *goal pyramid*. Here's how to do it:

1. Centered at the top of a piece of paper, write down what you hope to ultimately gain from

your education. This is your long-range goal
and the pinnacle of your pyramid. Example:
Become a successful advertising copywriter.

2. Below your long-range goal(s), list mid-
range goals—milestones or steps that will
lead you to your eventual target. For example, if your long-range goal were to become
an advertising copywriter, your mid-range
goals might include getting into college,
"acing" all your writing course, completing
all required courses and getting a summer
internship at a major ad agency.

3. Below the mid-range goals, list as many
short-range goals as you can—smaller steps
which can be completed in a relatively short
period of time. For example, if your long-
range goal is to become a travel writer for a
widely read magazine, your mid-range goal
may be to earn a degree in journalism.
Short-range goals may include writing a
travel article to submit to the school paper,
registering for magazine writing courses or
getting an excellent grade in a related class.

Change your goal pyramid as you progress through
school. You may eventually decide on a different career.
Or your mid-range goals may change as you decide on a
different path leading to the long-range goal. The short-
range goals will undoubtedly change, even daily.

The process of creating your own goal pyramid allows
you to see *how* all those little daily and weekly steps you
take can lead to your mid-range and long-term goals, and
will thereby motivate you to work on your daily and weekly
tasks with more energy and enthusiasm.

Make goal-setting a part of your life

The development of good study skills is the highway to your goals, whatever they are. And no matter how hard you have to work or how much adversity you have to overcome along the way, the journey will indeed be worth it.

How do you make goal setting a part of your life? Here are some hints I think will help you:

1. *Be realistic* when you set goals. Don't aim too high or too low and don't be particularly concerned when (not if) you have to make adjustments along the way.

2. *Be realistic* about your expectations. An improved understanding of a subject you have little aptitude for is preferable to getting hopelessly bogged down if total mastery of the subject is just not in the cards.

3. *Beware the Goldilocks Conundrum*—despite the previous two points, you can be *overly* realistic—too ready to sigh and give up just because something "isn't in the cards." There's a fine line between aiming too high and feeling miserable when you don't come close, aiming too low and never achieving your potential, and finding the path that's right for you.

4. *Concentrate on areas that offer the best chance for improvement.* Unexpected successes can do wonders for your confidence and might make it possible for you to achieve more than you thought in other areas.

5. *Monitor your achievements and keep resetting your goals.* Daily, weekly, monthly,

yearly—ask yourself how you've done and
where you'd like to go *now*.

Use rewards as artificial motivators

The way you decide to use a reward system all depends
on how much help you need getting motivated to study. As
we've observed, tasks that are intrinsically interesting require little outside motivation. However, most schoolwork
can be spurred along by the promise of little rewards along
the way. If the task is especially tedious or difficult, make
the rewards more frequent so that motivation doesn't sag.

As a general rule, the size of the reward should match
the difficulty of the task. For an hour of reading, promise
yourself a 10-minute walk. For completion of a rough draft
for a big assignment, treat yourself to a movie.

Carrot or stick?

In trying to motivate yourself, do you tend to use the
carrot or the stick? Positive and negative thoughts can both
motivate.

The following are examples of *negative* thoughts that
students have used to motivate themselves:

1. "If I don't get a good mark on this test, there
   goes my grade."
2. "If I don't finish this assignment, I'll have
   to miss the party."
3. "If I blow this college entrance exam, my
   future is shot."
4. "I'll be forced to go to summer school if I
   don't do well in this class."

Now here are some examples of *positive* thoughts that
students have used to motivate themselves:

1. "For every hour of solid study, I get to listen to two songs on my new CD."
2. "If I get this assignment done early, I will be able to go skiing Friday."
3. "If I earn an A in this class, I'll reward myself with a weekend at the beach."
4. "If I do well in these courses, my chances for grad school are excellent."

There is no rule against using the stick to motivate yourself. But, you should learn to turn your failures into successes. This will keep your attitude positive and keep the wind in your sails. Focusing on the positive helps you feel good about yourself and provides excitement to keep you motivated.

Creating *your* environment

The time is 9:30 p.m. A Metallica album is on the turntable, and it's cranked up. Your books and notes are strewn across the floor in no particular order. The History test is scheduled for 9 a.m. tomorrow and you haven't looked at the textbook in a week. You've promised your mother you'll take out the garbage and walk the dog. You were up late watching a favorite TV show last night and you're still tired.

With all these distractions, the noise level, other commitments and your general fatigue, you're not exactly heading for quality study time. And that's the point: Within such an environment, time spent will most likely be time wasted. How will you concentrate with loud music? How will you focus on the retention, recognition and recall process when your eyelids are kissing? Will you be called away at a critical moment to walk the dog?

Now imagine the following scenario: You've found a quiet corner at a reading table in your local library. You just left class and plan to review your History notes while they're still fresh in your mind. You look around you. All heads are down—focusing, concentrating, thinking. This is a *study* environment—you are not separated from the activities of others, but rather a willing participant in a seemingly universal pattern. Now you're ready for *quality* study time.

In half the time you had scheduled, you finish your reading, sift the material, make your notes and head for home.

This comparison of good and bad study environments is so simple as to be self-evident, you'd think. Amazingly, the negative situation portrayed is all too often the case. If it's one *you're* more familiar with, it's time to change. You need the right skills and the right environment if you are to be successful. But the right environment for you is probably the wrong one for someone else. Do you know where, when and how *you* study best?

In the library? At home? At a friend's?

Before dinner? After dinner?

When it's quiet? Noisy? With music? With the TV on?

Easiest assignments first? Hardest? Reading before writing?

Check it out

On page 37, I have included a checklist for you to rate your study environment. It includes not just *where* you study—at home, in the library, at a friend's—but *when* and *how* you study, too. Once you've identified what works for you, avoid those situations in which you now *know* you don't perform best. If you don't know the answer to one or more of the questions, take the time to experiment.

Blood Pressure/Lipid Profile Chart

Date						
Total Cholesterol						
Triglycerides						
HDL (good cholesterol)						
LDL (bad cholesterol)						
Cholesterol/ HDL Ratio						
Fasting Glucose						
Blood Pressure						

See reverse side for guidelines referenced from National Cholesterol Education Program
- Adult Treatment Panel III, American Diabetes Association and Joint National Committee
on Prevention, Detection, Evaluation, and Treatment of High Blood Pressure (JNC VII).

214095 07/03

MEDICATION LIST:

Name	Dosage

Allergies (medication, food, etc.)

_____

_____

_____

_____

Total Cholesterol
Less than 200mg/dL - Desirable
200 - 239mg/dL - Borderline high
240mg/dL and over - High

Triglycerides
Less than 150mg/dL - Desirable

HDL Cholesterol
Less than 40mg/dL - Low
60mg/dL and over - High

LDL Cholesterol
Less than 100mg/dL - Optimal
100 - 129mg/dL - Near/Above optimal
130 - 159mg/dL - Borderline high
160 - 189mg/dL - High
190mg/dL and over - Very high

Glucose
Less than 100 - Desirable
110 - 125 - Impaired
Greater than 126 - Diabetic

Blood Pressure
Less than 120/80mm Hg - Normal

My Ideal Study Environment

How I receive information best:

1. ❑ Orally ❑ Visually

In the classroom, I should:

2. ❑ Concentrate on taking notes ❑ Concentrate on listening
3. ❑ Sit in front ❑ Sit in back ❑ Sit near window or door

Where I study best:

4. ❑ At home ❑ In the library ❑ Somewhere else:
    _____

When I study best:

5. ❑ Every night; little on weekends ❑ Mainly on week-ends ❑ Spread out over seven days
6. ❑ In the morning ❑ Evening ❑ Afternoon
7. ❑ Before dinner ❑ After dinner

How I study best:

8. ❑ Alone ❑ With a friend ❑ In a group
9. ❑ Under time pressure ❑ Before I know I have to
10. ❑ With music ❑ In front of TV ❑ In a quiet room
11 ❑ Organizing an entire night's studying before I start
    ❑ Tackling and completing one subject at a time

I need to take a break:

12. ❑ Every 30 minutes or so ❑ Every hour ❑ Every 2 hrs.
    ❑ Every ____ hours

(For more information about creating the ideal study environment, be sure to read Chapter 3 in *Manage Your Time,* another of the five books in my new **HOW TO STUDY** *Program.)*

Many of the items on this chart should be understandable to you now. Remember: *Why* you feel the need for a particular environment is not important. Knowing that you *have a preference* is. Here's what you're trying to assess in each item:

1. If you prefer "listening" to "seeing," you'll have little problem getting the information you need from class lectures and discussion. In fact, you'll *prefer* them to studying your textbooks. (You may have to concentrate on your reading skills and spend more time with your textbooks to offset this tendency. Highlighting your texts may help.)

If you're more of a "visual" person, you'll probably find it easier reading your textbook and may have to work to improve your classroom concentration. Taking excellent class notes that you can read later will probably be important for you.

2. This should tie in with your answer to (1). The more "oral" you are, the more you should concentrate on listening. The more "visual," the better your notes should be for later review.

3. This may make a difference for a number of reasons. You may find it difficult to hear or see from the back of the classroom. You may be shy and want to sit up front to make yourself participate. You may find sitting near a window makes you feel less claustrophobic; alternatively, you may daydream too much if near a window and should sit as far "inside" the classroom as possible.

4. Whatever location you find most conducive to study —given the limitations of your living situation and

schedule—should be where you spend the majority of your study time.

5. How to organize your time to most effectively cover the material: This may depend, in part, on the amount of homework you are burdened with and/or the time of year —you may have one schedule during most of the school year but have to adapt during test time, if papers are due, for special projects, etc.

6. To some of you, such preferences may only be a factor on weekends, because your day hours are set—you're in school.

But if you're in college (or in a high school program that mimics college's "choose your own courses and times" scheduling procedures), you would want to use this factor in determining when to schedule your classes.

If you study best in the morning, for example, try to schedule as many classes as possible in the afternoons (or, at worst, late in the morning).

If you study best in the evening, either schedule morning classes and leave your afternoons free for other activities, or schedule them in the afternoons so you can sleep later (and study later the night before).

7. Some of us get cranky if we try to do *anything* when we're hungry. If you study poorly when your stomach is growling, eat something!

8. Most of us grow up automatically studying alone. If we "study with a friend," there's often more horseplay than studying. But don't underestimate the positive effect studying with one or two friends—or even a larger study group—can have on your mastery of schoolwork and on your grades.

I didn't really learn about study groups until a few years ago and never had the chance to participate in one. I certainly wish I had *(and* that I had started one in high school)—I realize now I could have saved myself a lot of work and taken advantage of the skills, expertise and minds of some of my brighter classmates.

9. Just because you perform best under pressure doesn't mean you should always leave projects, papers and studying for tests until the last minute. It just means if you're well organized, but an unexpected project gets assigned or a surprise test announced, you won't panic. If you do *not* study well under pressure, it certainly doesn't mean you occasionally won't be required to. The better organized you arc, tho easier it will be for you all the time, but especially when the unexpected arises.

10. As we've discussed, some of you (like me) will find it difficult to concentrate with*out* music or some sort of noise. Others couldn't sit in front of the TV and do *any*thing but breathe and eat.

Many of you will fall in between—you can read and even take notes to music but need absolute quiet to study for a test or master particularly difficult concepts. If you don't know how you function best, now is the time to find out.

11. Back to organizing. The latter concept—starting and finishing one project before moving on to another—doesn't mean you can't at least sit down and outline an entire night's study plan before tackling each subject, one at a time. Setting up such a study schedule *is* advised. But it may mean you really *can't* move to another project while the one you're now working on is unfinished. Others of you may have no problem working on one project, switching to another when you get stuck or just need a break, then going back to the first.

12. There's nothing particularly wrong with taking a break whenever you feel you need to to keep yourself sharp and maximize your quality study time...as long as the

breaks aren't every five minutes and don't last longer than the study periods! In general, though, try to increase your concentration through practice so that you can go at least an hour before getting up, stretching and having a drink or snack. Too many projects will require at least that long to "get into" or organize, and you may find that breaking too frequently will require too much "review time" when you return to your desk.

da Vincis are hard to find

It is the rare individual who is superior, or even good, in *every* subject. If you are, count your blessings. Most of us are a little better in one subject or another. Some of us simply *like* one subject more than another—and don't think *that* doesn't change your attitude toward it. Others are naturally gifted in one area, average in others.

For example, skill with numbers and spatial relations may come easily to you. but you may have no ear for music or languages. Or you may find learning a language to be easy, but not have the faintest clue why Pythagoras came up with his Theorem—or why you should care. Some students are good with their hands (or, as your career counselor would put it, "exhibit unusual motor skills"). Others (again, like me) may find making the simplest item akin to torture. So I'll never be known as "handy."

The reasons for such unequal distribution of native-born talents rest somewhere in the area between karma and God, depending on your philosophy.

Presuming that most of us are good in one or two subjects, average or poor in others, we can react to this state of affairs in one of two ways: 1) Concentrate on those areas in which we're weakest and work to improve basic skills such as reading, memory and organization so as to minimize our lack of particular talents; or 2) concentrate

exclusively on developing the particular skills we feel we
like or need without worrying about the others at all.

Most of you would probably lean to the former solution.
That's why you're plowing through this book, isn't it? And
the skills you will learn, practice and strengthen throughout it will undoubtedly change your approach to subjects
you currently dislike or just aren't good at. It will never
enable you to add a string of numbers in your head faster
than a calculator or start speaking a language with a
native accent just by listening to the waiter in the local
French restaurant. Unless those talents are in your
genes. But it may give you the impetus to do better in math
or learn French with a little less pain.

On the other hand, each of us has probably met someone who has taken the second course—strengthening his
or her native-born talents and ignoring the rest. Such a
person—salesman, computer guru, physician, etc.—may
have reached an incredible plateau of success in his or her
field. While being suitably impressed by their professional
accomplishments, we may be astounded at their demonstrated ignorance of literature, current affairs, art, music
or a number of other areas.

Should we criticize this person for concentrating solely
on his or her strengths and doing it so successfully that he
or she becomes a world-famous surgeon or the owner of a
billion-dollar computer firm? Even if he or she never did
do particularly well in English?

It's one way to get where you want to go. And may well
be a path you choose.

A word of caution

Before you agree with the conclusion that only God-
given talents are worthy of development, however, here's
some cautionary advice: Pursuit of such a goal can either

be a mixed blessing or a gift in disguise. Logic tells us that things that come easily can be easily achieved. Which is not to say that those areas that require more study cannot be mastered.

My advice is to be thankful for whatever native-born talents you possess and use the gift as a two edged sword. Shift some study time from those tasks easily achieved to those which you find more difficult. The balance you will see in your development will be well worth the effort.

And if you've never really thought about the subjects you like and dislike, use the chart on page 44 to identify them. You'll also be asked to identify those in which you perform well or poorly. (Your report card should confirm your list of those!) Use this list to organize your own schedule to take advantage of your natural talents and give added time to the subject areas that need the most work.

And if you have a choice

All college students—and some high school students— are able to pick and choose courses according to their own schedules, likes, dislikes, goals, etc. The headiness of such freedom should be tempered with the common-sense approach you're trying to develop through reading this book. Here are a few hints to help you along:

1. Whenever possible, consider each professor's reputation as you decide whether to select a particular course (especially if it is an overview or introductory course that is offered in two or three sessions). Word soon gets around as to which professors' lectures are stimulating and rewarding—an environment in which learning is a joy, even if it isn't a subject you like!

2. Attempt to select classes so that your schedule is balanced on a weekly and even a daily basis, though this will not always be possible or advisable. (Don't change

Evaluation of Subject Areas

List the subject areas/courses you like most:

_____

_____

_____

List those you like least:

_____

_____

_____

List the courses in which you get the best grades:

_____

_____

_____

And those in which you get the worst grades:

_____

_____

_____

your major just to fit your schedule!). Try to leave an open hour or half-hour between classes—it's ideal for review, post-class note taking, quick trips to the library, etc.

3. Try to alternate challenging classes with those that come more easily to you. Studying is a process of positive reinforcement. You'll need encouragement along the way.

4. Avoid late-evening or early-morning classes, especially if such scheduling provides you with large gaps of "down time."

5. Set a personal study pace and follow it. Place yourself on a study diet, the key rule of which is: *Don't overeat.*

The landscape is littered with the shadows of unsuccessful students who have failed in their pursuits—*not* because they lacked the talent or motivation, but because they just overloaded on information and pressure.

You *can* be successful without killing yourself!

Chapter 3

HOW TO
Read
And
Remember

"**H**e's well read."

"She's a reader."

"It's all in the books."

Such oft-quoted references accentuate the value of this amazing process by which we view the written page and sop up knowledge, mood, emotion, facts, story line, etc.

Reading transforms and transports us through times past, present and future.

Nothing you will do as you pursue your studies will be as valuable as the reading skills you develop—they are your ultimate long-term learning tool.

Presuming you agree, what do you do?

This chapter will help you learn:

- The standard sections of books designed to help you and how to use them
- How to read material the right way (three types of reading)
- How fast (or slow) you should be reading
- How to take better notes in your textbooks and during your reading assignments.
- How to comprehend more of what you read
- How your memory works and what you can do to improve it
- How to build your own library of books and authors

I can only cover so much in one chapter. After reading this one, if you feel you need more help with your reading comprehension, I urge you to consult *Improve Your Reading,* one of four brand-new books in my **HOW TO STUDY Program.**

The shorthand of reading

There is a group of special sections found in nearly all textbooks and technical materials (in fact, in almost all books except novels) that contain a wealth of information and can help you glean more from your reading. Becoming familiar with this data will enrich your reading experience and often make it easier. Here's what to look for:

The first page after the title page is usually the *Table of Contents*—a chapter-by-chapter list of the book's contents. Some are surprisingly detailed, listing every major point or topic covered in each chapter.

The first prose section (after the title page, table of contents and, perhaps, acknowledgements page, in which the author thanks other authors and his or her editor, typist, researcher, friends, relatives, teachers, etc., most of which can be ignored by the reader), the *Preface* is usually a description of what information you will find in the book. Authors may also use the preface to point out unique aspects of their books.

The *Introduction* may be in place of or in addition to the preface and may be written by the author or some "name" the author has recruited to lend additional prestige to his or her work. Most introductions are an even more detailed overview of the book—chapter-by-chapter summaries are often included to give the reader a feel for the material to be covered.

Footnotes may be found throughout the text (a slightly elevated number following a sentence, quote etc. (e.g., "jim dandy"[24]) and either explained at the bottom of the page on which they appear or in a special section at the back of the text. Footnotes may be used to cite sources of direct quotes or ideas and/or to further explain a point, add information, etc. outside of the text. You may make it a habit to ferret out sources cited in this way for further reading.

If a text tends to use an alarmingly high number of terms with which you may not be familiar, the considerate author will include a *Glossary*—essentially an abridged dictionary that defines all such terms.

The *Bibliography*, usually at the end of the book, may include the source material the author used to research the textbook, a list of "recommended reading" or both. It is usually organized alphabetically by subject, making it easy for you to go to your library and find more information on a specific topic.

Appendices containing supplementary data or examples relating to subject matter covered in the text may also appear in the back of the book.

The last thing in a book is usually the *Index,* an alphabetical listing that references, by page number, every mention of a particular name, subject, topic, etc. in the text.

Making it a habit to utilize all of these tools in your textbooks can only make your studying easier.

Three ways to read

Depending on what you're trying to accomplish in a particular reading assignment and the kind of book involved, there are actually three different ways to read. Knowing when to use each will make any assignment easier:

1. *Quick reference reading* focuses on seeking specific information that addresses a particular question or concern we might have;

2. *Critical reading* is used to discern ideas and concepts that require a thorough analysis;

2. *Aesthetic or pleasure reading,* which we do for sheer entertainment or to appreciate an author's style and ability.

Skim first, then read for detail

The best way to begin any reading assignment is to skim the pages to get an overall view of what information is included. Then scan and highlight the text and/or take notes in your notebook.

Newspapers make reading simple—most newspaper articles are written in the "pyramid" format. The first paragraph (at the top of the pyramid) makes the major point of the story. Succeeding paragraphs add more and more detail, filling out the pyramid. So gleaning the key news stories from a newspaper is as easy as reading the headlines and the first two or three paragraphs of each.

Your textbooks are not always written to facilitate such an approach, but most of the authors probably make their key point of any paragraph in the first sentence of that paragraph. Succeeding sentences add details. In addition, most of your textbooks include helpful "call outs"—those brief notes or headings in the outside margins of each page that summarize the topic covered in the paragraph or section. Or, like this book, include headings and sub-headings to organize the material.

These standard organizational tools should make your reading job simpler. The next time you have to read a history, geography or similar text, try skimming the assigned pages first. Read the heads, the subheads and the call outs. Read the first sentence of each paragraph. Then go back and start reading the details.

To summarize the skimming process:

1. Read and be sure you understand the title or heading. Try rephrasing it as a question for further clarification of what you will read.

2. Examine all the subheadings, illustrations, and graphics—these will help you identify the significant matter within the text.

3. Read *thoroughly* the introductory paragraphs, the summary at the end and any questions at chapter's end.

4. Read the first sentence of every paragraph— this generally includes the main idea.

5. Evaluate what you have gained from this process: Can you answer the questions at the end of the chapter? Could you intelligently participate in a class discussion of the material?

6. Write a brief summary that capsulizes what you have learned from your skimming.

7. Based on this evaluation, decide whether a more thorough reading is required.

Now go back for detail

If a more thorough reading is then required, turn back to the beginning. *Read one section (chapter, etc.) at a time.* And do not go on to the next until you've completed the following exercise:

1. Write definitions of any key terms you feel are essential to understanding the topic.

2. Write questions and answers you feel clarify the topic.

3. Write any questions for which you *don't* have answers—then make sure you find them through re-reading, further research or asking another student or your teacher.

4. Even if you still have unanswered questions, move on to the next section and complete numbers 1-3 for that section. (And so on, until your reading assignment is complete.)

See if this method doesn't help you get a better handle on any assignment right from the start.

Reading technical texts

Math and science texts (or any highly technical ones, like economics) require slightly different handling. Steps 1 through 3 should still be followed, with one addition: Make sure you understand the concepts expressed in the various graphs or charts.

And do *not proceed* to step 4. You must understand one section before moving on to the next, since the next concept is usually based on the previous one. If there are sample problems, go and solve those that tie in with the section you have just read to make sure you understand the concepts imparted. If you still fail to grasp a key concept, equation, etc., start again and try again. But *don't* move on—you'll just be wasting your time.

Reading foreign language texts

Foreign language texts should be approached the same way, especially basic ones teaching vocabulary. If you haven't mastered the words you're supposed to in the first section, you'll have trouble reading the story at the end of section three, even if you've learned all the words in sections two and three. So take it one step at a time and make sure you have mastered one concept, vocabulary list, lesson, etc. before jumping ahead.

Aesthetic (pleasure) reading

> To read a writer is for me not merely to get an idea of what he says, but to go off with him, and travel in his company.
> — Andre Gide

This is the kind of reading you do for pure enjoyment, for diversion, for the appreciation of a certain literary style or tone. Of course, the great works, from **War and Peace** to **Wuthering Heights**, can also be enjoyed as pleasure reading. But if you're reading for an English or Literature class, you'll probably want to combine the aesthetic method with the critical method.

Most fiction is an attempt to tell a story. There is a beginning, in which characters and setting are introduced.

There is a conflict or struggle that advances the story to a climax—where the conflict is resolved. A final *denouement* or "winding up" unravels or clarifies the conclusion of the story.

Your literature class will address all of these parts using literary terms that are often more confusing than helpful. The following are brief definitions of some of the more important ones:

> *Plot:* The order or sequence of the story—how it proceeds from opening through climax. Your ability to understand and appreciate literature depends upon how well you follow the plot—the *story.*

> *Characterization:* The personalities or characters central to the story—the heroes, the heroines and the villains. You will want to identify the main characters of the story and their relationship to the struggle or conflict. Pay particular attention as to whether the characters are three dimensional—are they real and believable?

> *Theme:* The controlling message or subject of the story, the moral or idea that the author is using the plot and characters to communicate. Some examples: man's inhumanity to man, man's impotency in his environment, the corrupting influence of power, greed and unrequited love. You need to discern this theme to really understand what it is the author wants to communicate.

> *Setting:* The time and place in which the story takes place. This is especially important when reading a historical novel or one that takes you to another culture.

Point of View: Who is telling the story? Is it one of the central characters giving you flashbacks or a first-person perspective? Or is it a third-person narrator offering commentary and observations on the characters, the setting and the plot? This is the person who moves the story and gives it an overall tone.

The first step in reading literature is to familiarize yourself with these concepts—then to try to recognize them in the novel or short story. Then, begin your reading, approaching it first from an aesthetic standpoint: How does it make you feel? What do you think of the characters? Do you like them? Hate them? Relate to them?

Second, make sure you know what's going on—this involves the plot or story line and the development of the characters. On a chapter-by-chapter basis, you may find it helpful to keep a sheet of paper on which you can jot a sentence or two of the plot development (and, if you wish, characters introduced, etc.). For example, your notes on the first chapter of *The Time Machine* by H. G Wells might read:

Time Traveller, Psychologist, the Provincial Mayor, the Medical Man, a Very Young Man and Filby are in the Time Traveller's house. It is a winter evening (fire is going). They talk about the geometry of Four Dimensions—4th dimension is time. TT declares he has discovered way to move about in Time and shows them experimental verification—small model for Time Machine (took two yrs to make) that disappears when activated. Claims it is travelling in time. Announces that big machine is nearly ready and, when finished, he will use it for a journey in Time.

I have written these notes out, but obviously you would not need to do so. Simply listing the points in outline fashion or noting key words would be sufficient.

Does this adequately summarize the first chapter so you wouldn't have to read it? Not really. Yes, it tells you the characters introduced and, in bare-bones fashion, what happened.

But it leaves out all of the details of the philosophical debate that begins the book and, most importantly, cannot possibly capture the mystery, foreboding and thrill of entering an adventure that Wells manages to convey in this single chapter. And it leaves out important information like the themes carried out in the book, use of literary devices, etc.

To truly summarize this chapter, you might label the above paragraph "Plot," then include separate notes under the headings "Themes" and "Literary." This would certainly help you both understand what you've read and simplify your review task come test time.

Take out the crayolas

If you have a desk drawer full of magic markers *(aka highlighters),* you're probably already familiar with the process of underlining text. It can be a useful method for zeroing in on what's important, both during the classroom preparation stage and when you're compiling your notes. But be careful that in your quest to highlight pertinent information, you don't end up with your entire reading assignment in yellow.

The other danger of highlighting is that you tend not to pay as much attention to what you're reading as you underline your material. If you're not comfortable reading without your yellow marker, please keep this advice in mind:

1. Underlining should identify words or sentences that capsulize a section's major ideas or themes.

2. Underlining should indicate the relative importance of things, allowing you to concentrate your review time on key words, facts and concepts (underlined) and skip the digressions, examples and extraneous explanations (not underlined).

To sharpen your underlining skills, read though the next three paragraphs and indicate with your highlighter which information you feel is important:

> For the most part, young people entering the field do not understand just what public relations involves or how to employ public relations techniques to address a communications issue. Some think it involves just dealing with the press. Others think it is mostly writing. Still others are sure that whatever it is, it's involved somehow with affecting public opinion, but then confuse it with advertising.
>
> In fact, public relations might be defined in many ways. *Webster's New World Dictionary* defines it as "those functions of a corporation concerned with informing the public of its activities, policies, etc., and attempting to create favorable public opinion." Other texts have used slightly different definitions.
>
> We tell anyone interested in public relations that the best way to understand the field is to intern in either a public relations firm or a corporate communications department of a major company. This will give you firsthand experience and exposure to the many varied facets of public relations *before* you have to commit yourself to the field.

It should be obvious that the definition of public relations is the essence of the first two paragraphs. You'll want to remember "those functions of a corporation... favorable public opinion." Highlight that entire definition. (If this were in one of your textbooks, you may want to write in the margin "PR: def" as a way of catching your attention and moving your eye to this important information.

Secondly, you may highlight the word "intern" or even the whole phrase "best way to understand the field is to intern," the key point in the third paragraph.

Now if you had to review that book for a test, you would glance at two sentences—the two you highlighted—to get the gist of three paragraphs.

How fast can you understand?

> When we read too fast or too slowly, we understand nothing.
> — Pascal

Are you worried that you read too slowly? You probably shouldn't be—less-rapid readers are not necessarily less able. What counts is what you comprehend and remember. And like anything else, practice will probably increase your speed levels. If you must have a ranking, take any randomly selected text of 250 words and read it from start to finish, noting the elapsed time on your watch. Then score yourself as follows:

Under 20 seconds	Very Fast
21-30 secs.	Fast
31-45 secs	Average
46-60 secs.	Slow
61+ secs.	Very Slow

You should only worry—and plan to do something about it—if you fall in the slow or very slow range. Unless you do, you are probably reading as fast as you need to. Again, the relationship between your reading speed and your comprehension is paramount: Read too fast and you may comprehend less; reading slowly does not necessarily mean you're not grasping the material. There are several things you can do to improve these reading mechanics.

To increase your reading speed:

1. Focus your attention and concentration.
2. Eliminate outside distractions.
3. Provide for an uncluttered, comfortable environment.
4. Don't get hung up on single words or sentences, but *do* look up (in the dictionary) key words that you must understand in order to grasp an entire concept.
5. Try to grasp overall concepts rather than attempting to understand every detail.

To increase comprehension:

1. Try to make the act of learning sequential—comprehension is built by adding new knowledge to existing knowledge.
2. Review and re-think at designated points in your reading. Test yourself to see if the import of the material is getting through.
3. If things don't add up, discard your conclusions. Go back, reread and try to find an alternate conclusion.

4. Summarize what you've read, rephrasing it
in your notes, in your own words.

Most importantly, read at the speed that's comfortable
for you. Though I *can* read extremely fast, I *choose* to read
novels much more slowly so I can appreciate the author's
word play. Likewise, any material that I find particularly
difficult to grasp slows me right down. I read newspapers,
popular magazines and the like very fast, seeking to grasp
the information but not worrying about every detail.

Should you take some sort of speed reading course,
especially if your current speed level is slow? I can't see
that it could particularly hurt you in any way. I can also,
however, recommend that you simply keep practicing
reading, which will increase your speed naturally.

Remembering what you read

In a world where the ability to master and remember a
growing explosion of data is critical for individual success, too little attention is paid to the dynamics of memory
and systems for improving it. Developing your memory is
probably the most effective way to increase your efficiency,
in reading and virtually everything else.

Retention

Retention is the process by which we keep imprints of
past experiences in our minds, the "storage depot." Subject
to other actions of the mind, what is retained can be re-
called when needed.

Things are retained in the same order in which they
are learned. So your studying should build one fact, one
idea, one concept upon another.

Broad concepts can be retained easier than details.
Master the generalities and the details will fall into place.

If you think something is important, you will retain it more easily. So convincing yourself that what you are studying is something you must retain (and recall) increases your chances of adding it to your storehouse.

Recall

This is the process by which we are able to bring forth those things that we have retained. Recall is subject to strengthening through the process of repetition. *Recall is least effective immediately after a first reading*, emphasizing the importance of review. The dynamics of our ability to recall are affected by several factors.

We most easily recall those things that are of interest to us.

Be selective in determining how much you need to recall. All information is not of equal importance—focus your attention on being able to recall the most *important* pieces of information.

Allow yourself to react to the data you are studying. Being able to associate new information with what you already know will make it easier to recall.

Repeat, out loud or just in your mind, what you want to remember. Find new ways of saying those things that you want to recall.

Try to recall broad concepts rather than isolated facts.

Use the new data you have managed to recall in a meaningful way—it will help you recall it the next time.

Recognition

This is the ability to see new material and recognize it for what it is and what it means. Familiarity is the key aspect of recognition—you will feel that you have "met" this information before, associate it with other data or circumstances and then recall the framework in which it logically fits.

If you've ever envied a friend's seemingly wondrous ability to recall facts, dates, telephone numbers, etc. virtually at will, take solace that, in most cases, *this skill is a result of study and practice,* not something anyone is born with.

There are certain fundamental memory systems that, when mastered, can significantly expand your capability. It is beyond the scope of this book to teach you these detailed techniques, but if you feel you need help, why not consult your local library? I personally recommend a best seller from a few years ago called **The Memory Book** by Harry Lorayne and Jerry Lucas, but I'm sure you'll find a number of helpful titles at your library.

Test your reading comprehension

Remember: Comprehending what you read is, to a great extent, more important than how fast you read it. The following section will test your reading comprehension. The first selection is the easiest, the following two progressively more difficult. Read each selection carefully, then answer the questions. And note that there is not necessarily a single right answer for each question, only one closest to the truth.

Fiction (least difficult)

David approached the house slowly. An attitude of caution overcame him as without prior knowledge, just what he could expect to find was problematic. Communications with the old man and woman had been sparse and in recent years very few words of their welfare had come to the family.

Economic conditions in that part of the world were just beginning to stabilize. The first Great War and now this revolution cast a doubt on one's ability to eke out even the most meager of existences. He had come prepared with a gift of dollars, which he knew would help to guarantee their welfare.

Finally he arrived at the door and within a moment the three of them were embracing. How strange, he thought, the way the bonds of family could bridge oceans. Immediately he realized he belonged and that his long journey had indeed been the right thing to do.

Questions (choose only one answer)

1. In this fictional account, the writer's primary purpose is to:

    A. Give the reader a view of economic conditions

    B. Describe the difficulties of meeting long-lost relatives

    C. Emphasize the bonds of family that remain regardless of circumstance

    D. Pad the book by another page

    E. Demonstrate that virtue is its own reward

2. Where is the book set?

    A. Asia

    B. The United States

    C. Unknown

    D. Not the United States

    E. Heaven

3. What relation is David to the people he is visiting?

    A. They are his parents

B. They are his grandparents
C. They are family friends
D. They are relatives
E. They are people he met on the Road to Morocco

History (more difficult)

Franklin Delano Roosevelt's chief accomplishments encompass both domestic and international activities.

First elected when the country suffered a severe economic collapse, he was instrumental in mobilizing the nation's people and resources to spearhead a recovery. In present-day economic terms, he presided over the greatest turnaround in the nations' history.

Applying the full weight of central government, he established the principle of government as the court of last resort. Specifically this welfare approach included: the establishment of Social Security; a variety of "make-work" projects that created millions of jobs; federally guaranteed insurance on depositors' bank accounts; stock market regulation; rural power and electrification; the establishment of minimum wage and working conditions standards; and unemployment insurance.

During World War II, FDR presided over the largest military buildup and subsequent engagement ever faced by the nation. He was the successful Commander-In-Chief directing the military forces of the nation in a global encounter with the forces of Fascism.

Roosevelt, early on, recognized the threat the Axis powers presented and mobilized the country—primarily by helping to arm England via the mechanism of Lend-Lease—against them. There were those, and many in high places, who sought to minimize the American role in the impending war. Roosevelt, however, was accurate in his belief in the inevitability of U.S. involvement. He recognized the ultimate threat to American freedom that Fascism represented. When the Japanese attack on Pearl Harbor made war a *fait accompli,* Roosevelt was ready.

Roosevelt's wartime stewardship demonstrated, as it had during the Depression, his genius for leadership. His words mobilized the nation. His efforts, together with those of Stalin and Churchill, led the Free World to victory.

Some revisionist historians would argue that postwar activities (started at the Yalta Conference) jeopardized America's postwar influence, particularly in Eastern Europe. It seems more logical to assume the Cold War rivalry was a natural outgrowth of two antithetical systems, each feeling heady with victory, each determined to make their manner of governing the law of the land.

Roosevelt's place in history is assured. Though himself privileged by birth, he displayed an unusual compassion for the average man. A non-combatant because of his illness, he demonstrated a courage and leadership which stood as a fine example for battlefield troops.

Questions

1. The writer's main purpose in this selection is to:

   A. Describe world conditions during FDR's presidency.

   B. Demonstrate Roosevelt's grasp of both domestic and international problems.

   C. Indicate that leadership is essential for an effective presidency.

   D. Indicate the broad scope of programs developed to reinvigorate a depressed economy.

E. Emphasize the inevitability of confrontation between countries with different forms of government.

2. The author asserts that Roosevelt:

  A. Provided necessary leadership in turning the economy around.
  B. Did not hesitate to involve government.
  C. Was the grandfather of the welfare state.
  D. Pioneered many social reforms and make-work programs.

3. One can conclude that Roosevelt:

  A. Understood the real threat posed by Fascism.
  B. Was able to marshal the necessary cooperation among allies for the conduct of a successful global war effort.
  C. Understood the necessity to arm England.
  D. Was not anxious for war but realistic about its possibility.

4. The phrase "postwar influence" refers directly to:

  A. Agreement on spheres of power determined at Yalta.
  B. An acknowledgement of the military realities when hostilities ceased.
  C. The recognition of the competing natures of Democracy and Communism.
  D. A permanent division of the world along superpower lines.

Current events (most difficult)

The problem of the budget deficit will probably be one of the most difficult (and politically thorny) which the new Bush Administration will have to face.

Deficits in Federal budgets arise when expenditures exceed revenue receipts. The difference is considered the deficit.

Deficits cause problems because the dollars required to cover such budgetary shortfalls have to be borrowed. As on any loan, interest payments on the amount borrowed must also be made (debt service). With an annual deficit in the $100-200 billion range, it's easy to see how costly and non-productive such debt service payments can become.

Budget deficits are not a new problem and, some say, not even an important one. These latter optimists argue that the U. S. budget deficit is not the highest of all nations in the West, and, with everything being relative, it is not, therefore, a vital threat.

Whether or not you agree with this rosy scenario, the political impetus to reduce the deficit and ultimately live within our means is underway. Congress has crystalized this process by passing the Gramm-Rudman Act, a bill that mandates across-the-board budget cuts to meet certain deficit reduction targets. This is the law of the land, and it will be automatically exercised unless minimum reductions are effected voluntarily.

There are two favorite approaches now in play with respect to this balancing act:

Growth: This theory posits that the economy will grow with sufficient vigor to bring in sufficient increases in tax revenues to cover the shortfall.

Spending Cuts: Extensive cuts in social and military budgets, coupled with greater income tax revenues, will be required to cover the deficit.

The Administration has complicated the negotiating process between Congress and the Executive Branch with its campaign pledge to refrain from any new taxes. Read his lips.

The outlook is for a lengthy debate and some compromise agreement between the protagonists. Most political experts expect the process to go down to the wire, just shy of the Gramm-Rudman deadline.

Public opinion soundings indicate that, given a compelling case for the imposition of new taxes, the public is more willing to pay additional taxes than Congress is to push them.

Questions

1. The author characterizes budget deficits as:

    A. An unambiguous danger to the economy
    B. A subject of controversy and divided opinion
    C. The target of political jockeying
    D. Subject to adjustment

2. It is obvious from this reading that:

    A. Negotiating in good faith will be important
    B. Gramm-Rudman is a popular option
    C. Military cutbacks are on the table
    D. Bush's "no new taxes" pledge may backfire

3. Growing out of a deficit position:

    A. Is an optimist's point of view
    B. Threatens inflation
    C. Can be part of the solution
    D. Depends on realistic forecasting

4. People are willing to pay increased taxes:
   A. Reluctantly
   B. If a legitimate case can be made for them
   C. If they are progressive
   D. If they think they will get something in return

5. Budget deficits are:
   A. Like paying off a loan
   B. Non-productive vis a vis the interest paid on them
   C. An operating fact of life for most nations
   D. Possibly not a bad thing at all

Now check your answers on page 73. This is the kind of testing material you'll come upon again and again, and practice *does* make perfect. If you didn't get at least nine of these dozen questions right, work on your memory skills and start highlighting text as you read to make comprehension of the main points easier.

Did you have to read the entire text of each selection more than once to get the meaning? Did you find yourself reading more slowly than usual? Did it take you more than three minutes to read any of the texts?

If you answered "yes" to *any* of these questions, stop patting yourself on the back and start working on what you still need to improve—comprehension *with* speed.

Read on

Insofar as one can in a single chapter, I've tried to sum up the essentials of reading. It is not a finite science but rather a skill and appreciation that one can develop over time. Good grade school training is essential. And for those of you who have been able to identify problem areas, there are always remedial classes.

Having a "love affair" with books is the best boost you can give yourself. Reading is active, not passive. To paraphrase Timothy Leary: "Turn on, tune in, read a book."

Build a library

> The reading of all good books is like conversation with the finest men of past centuries.
> — Descartes

If you are ever to become an active, avid reader, access to books will do much to cultivate the habit. I suggest you "build" your own library. Your selections can and should reflect your own tastes and interests, but try to make them wide and varied. Include some of the classics, contemporary fiction, poetry and biography.

Save your high school and college texts—you'll be amazed at how some of the material retains its relevance. And try to read a good newspaper every day so as to keep current and informed.

Your local librarian can refer you to any number of lists of the "Great Books," most of which are available in inexpensive paperback editions. Here are three more lists—my own—of: 1) the "great" classical authors; 2) the "great" not-so-classical authors, poets and playwrights; and 3) a selection of my own "great books."

You may want to incorporate these on your buy list, especially if you're planning a summer reading program.

(Note: I'm sure I have left off someone's favorite author or "important" title from these lists. So be it. They are not meant to be comprehensive, just relatively representative. I doubt anyone would disagree that a person familiar with the majority of authors and works listed would be considered well-read!)

Some "great" classical authors

Boccaccio	Confucius	S. Johnson	Flaubert
Emerson	Kant	Spinoza	Rousseau
Aesop	Dante	Homer	Voltaire
Aquinas	Descartes	Horace	Shakespeare
Cervantes	Machiavelli	Nietzsche	Vergil
Chaucer	Goethe	Plato	Ovid
Aristotle	Dewey	Aeschylus	Santayana
J. Caesar	Erasmus	Milton	Swift
Balzac	Hegel	Montaigne	Pindar
Cicero	Aristophanes	Plutarch	Burke

Some other "great" authors

Albert Camus	Ellery Queen
Aldous Huxley	E. M. Forster
Aleksandr I. Solzhenitsyn	Emile Zola
Alexandre Dumas	Emily Bronte
Anthony Burgess	Emily Dickinson
Arthur Conan Doyle	Erich Maria Remarque
Bertolt Brecht	Ernest Hemingway
Bertrand Russell	Eugene O'Neill
Brendan Behan	Ezra Pound
Carl Sandburg	F. Scott Fitzgerald
Charles Dickens	Feodor Dostoevsk1
Charles Lamb	George Bernard Shaw
Charlotte Bronte	George Eliot
Daniel Defoe	George Orwell
D. H. Lawrence	George Sand
Dylan Thomas	Gertrude Stein
e e cummings	Henry Miller
Edgar Allan Poe	H W Longfellow
Edna Ferber	Hermann Hesse
Edward Albee	Herman Melville

H. G. Wells
H. H. Munro (Saki)
H. L. Mencken
James Baldwin
James Jones
James Joyce
James Russell Lowell
James Thurber
J. D. Salinger
Jean Paul Sartre
John Galsworthy
John Hersey
John Keats
John Updike
Jose Ortega y Gasset
Joseph Conrad
Joseph Heller
J. R. R. Tolkien
Leo Tolstoy
Lewis Carroll
Lillian Hellman
Lord Byron
Marcel Proust
Mark Twain
Maxim Gorki
Nathaniel Hawthorne
O. Henry
Oscar Wilde
Pearl Buck
Percy Bysshe Shelley

P. G. Wodehouse
Robert Frost
Robert Heinlein
Robert Louis Stevenson
Robert Penn Warren
Rudyard Kipling
Samuel Beckett
Saul Bellow
Sinclair Lewis
Tennessee Williams
Theodore Dreiser
Thomas Hardy
Thomas Mann
Thomas Wolfe
Thornton Wilder
Truman Capote
T. S. Eliot
Upton Sinclair
Victor Hugo
Vladimir Nabokov
Walt Whitman
Washington Irving
W. H. Auden
William Blake
William Butler Yeats
William Faulkner
William James
William Styron
William Wordsworth
W. Somerset Maugham

Some "great" works (in no particular order)

Animal Farm
Tom Jones

A Streetcar Named Desire
Look Homeward, Angel

Aesop's Fables

Alice In Wonderland

An American Tragedy

Arrowsmith

Canterbury Tales

Babbitt

The Bell Jar

Brave New World

The Brothers Karamazov

Catch-22

Grapes of Wrath

Don Juan

Death of a Salesman

The Deerslayer

The Great Gatsby

Lord Jim

Don Quixote

Wuthering Heights

Ethan Fromme

A Farewell to Arms

Gulliver's Travels

Hamlet

Huckelberry Finn

The Iliad

Kim

"Leaves of Grass"

Les Miserables

MacBeth

Main Street

The Merchant of Venice

Moby Dick

Native Son

1984

Of Human Bondage

Of Mice and Men

Oliver Twist

The Pickwick Papers

Othello

Our Town

War and Peace

"Paradise Lost"

Anna Karenina

Robinson Crusoe

Scarlet Letter

Siddhartha

The Magic Mountain

Silas Marner

Lady Chatterley's Lover

Steppenwolf

Demian

Tender Is the Night

Pride and Prejudice

The Catcher in the Rye

Bonfire of the Vanities

The Count of Monte Cristo

Crime and Punishment

The Federalist Papers

For Whom the Bell Tolls

The Foundation

The Thin Red Line

The Good Earth

David Copperfield

The Idiot

King Lear

The Invisible Man

Jane Eyre

The Lord of the Rings

The Prophet

"The Raven"   Tom Sawyer
Mother Courage   Romeo and Juliet
Return of the Native   Ulysses
The Sun Also Rises   Man and Superman
A Tale of Two Cities
The Time Machine   Vanity Fair
The Aeneid   Walden
"The Wasteland"   Heart of Darkness
The Trial   Julius Caesar

A Long Day's Journey Into Night
The Red Badge of Courage
"The Road Not Taken"
The Hound of the Baskervilles
One Flew Over the Cuckoo's Nest
Far From the Madding Crowd
The Legend of Sleepy Hollow
The Old Man and the Sea
Remembrance of Things Past
All Quiet On The Western Front
A Portrait of the Artist as a Young Man

Reading every one of these books will probably make you a better reader; it will certainly make you more well-read. And that is the extra added bonus to establishing such a reading program—an appreciation of certain authors, certain books, certain cultural events and the like is what separates the cultured from the merely educated and the undereducated. Read on and enjoy!

Answers to this chapter's comprehension quizzes: Fiction—1) C; 2) C; 3) D. History—1) B; 2) A; 3) A; 4) A. Current Events—1) D; 2) A; 3) D; 4) B; 5) B.

Chapter 4

HOW TO
Organize
Your
Time

We all have problems with time.

We can't control it or slow it down.

We need more of it. And don't know where to find it.

Then we wonder where it went.

But *time* is not really the problem. Time, after all, is the one "currency" that all people are given in equal supply, every day. The problem is that most of us simply let too much of it "slip through our fingers"—because we have *never been taught how to* manage *our time*. Our parents never sat us down to give us a little "facts of time" talk. And time management skills aren't part of any standard academic curriculum.

Whether you're a book author typing as fast as he can to meet the publisher's deadline, or a student juggling five classes and a part-time job, a simple, easy-to-follow time management system is crucial to your success.

In this chapter, we'll develop a time management plan for an entire term, learn how to prioritize tasks, and then create our daily schedules.

Collect what you need

As you begin your planning session, make sure you have all of the information and materials you need to make a quality plan. Gather your class syllabuses, work schedule, dates of important family events, vacations or trips, other personal commitments (doctor appointments, parties) and a calendar of any extracurricular events in which you plan to participate.

Keeping track of your day-to-day activities—classes, appointments, regular daily homework assignments and daily or weekly quizzes—will be dealt with after we talk about those projects—studying for mid-terms and finals, term papers, theses, etc.—that require completion over a long period. Weeks. Maybe even months.

Creating your Project Board

There are two excellent tools you can use for your long-term planning. The first is a Project Board, which you can put on any blank wall or right above your desk.

You can buy a ready-made chart at an art supply, stationery or bookstore. Or you can copy the format of the one I've included on pp. 76 and 77.

How does the Project Board work? As you can see, it is just a variation on a calendar. I have set it up vertically— the months running down the left-hand side, the projects across the top. You can switch the order if you want. (Many "store-bought" charts come set up this way.)

Sample Projects Board

MONTH/WEEK		PROJECT: STUDENT CORPORATION
1st MONTH	Week 1	Initial group meeting: Discuss overall assignment and possible products or services—bring list of three each to meeting (1 hour)
	Week 2	Finalize product or service; finalize organization of group and longterm responsibilities of each subgroup. (3)
	Week 3	Subgroup planning and short-term assignments (2)
	Week 4	Work on individual assignment from subgroup (?)
2nd MONTH	Week 1	Work on individual assignment from subgroup (?)
	Week 2	Work on individual assignment from subgroup (?)
	Week 3	Integrate individual assignment with rest of subgroup (?)
	Week 4	Meet with entire group to integrate plans (?)
3rd MONTH	Week 1	Finalize all-group plan; draft initial report (?)
	Week 2	Type and proof final report (?)
	Week 3	
	Week 4	
	DUE DATE	3RD MONTH/end of Week 2

PROJECT: DANTE TERM PAPER	REVIEW/EXAM SCHEDULE
Finalize topic (1 hour)	Review prior month's History notes (3)
Initial library research (2) General outline (1)	Review prior month's English notes (2)
Detailed library research (3) Detailed library research (3)	Review prior month's Science notes (4) Review prior month's Math notes (4)
Detailed library research (3) Detailed outline (1) First draft (4), Additional research (2)	Review 1st MONTH History notes (3) Review 1st MONTH English notes (2) Review 1st MONTH Science notes (4) Review 1st MONTH Math notes (4)
Second draft, spellcheck, proof (10) Independent proof (1) Type final draft and proof (4)	2nd MONTH History notes (3) 2nd MONTH English notes (2) 2nd MONTH Science notes (4) 2nd MONTH Math notes (4)
end of 3RD MONTH	end of 3RD MONTH

Using your Project Board

In the case of each project, there is a key preparatory step before you can use the chart: You have to break down each general assignment into its component parts. So, for example, in the case of an English report on Dante that just got assigned, we have identified the steps as:

1. Finalize topic
2. Initial library research
3. General outline
4. Detailed library research
5. Detailed outline
6. First draft
7. Second draft
8. Check spelling and proofread
9. Get someone else to proofread
10. Type final draft
11. Proofread again.
12. Turn in!

Next to each specific task, we have estimated the time we would expect to spend on it. (For more information about the steps required to writing a term paper, see chapter 7 in this book and read *Write Papers*, another of the books in my brand-new *HOW TO STUDY Program.*)

The second project involves working on a team with other students from your entrepreneurship class to create a hypothetical student business. While the steps are different, you'll notice that the concept of breaking the project down into separate and manageable steps and allocating time for each doesn't change.

However, because time allocation in later steps depends on what assignments you're given by the group, we have had to temporarily place question marks next to some steps. As the details of this project become clearer and specific assignments are made, your Project Board should be changed to reflect both more details and the specific time required for each step.

You should also include on your Project Board time for studying for all your final exams. If you have skipped ahead and read Chapter 8, you know that cramming for tests doesn't work very well in the short term and doesn't work at all over the long term. So you have taken my advice in that chapter and made it a habit to review your class notes on each subject on a monthly basis. You've decided that every Sunday morning is "review time" and allocated one Sunday a month to review the previous month's work in each subject.

As a result of this plan, you'll notice there is little time allocated to "last-minute" cramming or even studying for a specific final the week before it is given—just a couple of hours to go over any details you're still a little unsure of or to spend on areas you think will be on the test. While others are burning the midnight oil in the library the night before each exam, you're getting a good night's sleep and will enter the tests refreshed, relaxed and confident. Seems like a better plan to me.

As a byproduct of this study schedule, by the way, you will find that salient facts and ideas will remain with you long after anybody is testing you on them.

You have your Project Board. What do you do with it?

Keep adding any other important projects throughout the term and continue to revise it according to actual time spent as opposed to time allocated. Getting into this habit will make you more aware of how much time to allocate to future projects and make sure that the more you do so, the more accurate your estimates will be.

Month	Mon	Tue	Wed	Thu	Fri	Sat	Sun
Feb	18	19	20	21	22	23	24
	25	26	27 conference 4-5	28	1	2	3
March	4	5	6	7	8 Afternoon: A.A.P. meeting	9	10
	11 sociology Presentation	12	13 Math: Ch.1-3	14	15	16	17 Trip Home
	18	19	20 Math: Ch 4	21	22	23	24

Month	Mon	Tue	Wed	Thu	Fri	Sat	Sun
	25	26	27 Math: Ch.5	28	29	30	31
April	1	2	3 No Math Due	4	5	6	7 — Trip to Jim & Dana's
	8	9	10 Math: Ch. 6-8	11	12 Sociology Paper due!	13	14
	15 Biology Lab Journal Due!!	16 Last day of class	17	18	19	20 Biology Final 3:00	21
	22 Math Final 2:00	23	24	25 ← CAMPING !!!	26 ☺	27	28 →

Using a Term Planning Calendar

The Term Planning Calendar, an example of which is shown on pp. 80 and 81, can be used in concert with or in place of the Project Board. (There's a blank form on p. 97)

To use it with the Project Board, start by transferring all the information from the Project Board to your Term Planning Calendar. Then add your weekly class schedule, work schedule, family celebrations, vacations and trips, club meetings and extracurricular activities. Everything. The idea is to make sure your Calendar has *all* the scheduling information, while your Project Board contains just the briefest summary that you can ingest at a glance.

Leave your Project Board on your wall at home; carry your Term Planning Calendar with you. Whenever new projects, appointments, meetings, etc. are scheduled, add them immediately to your Calendar. Then transfer the steps involving major projects to your Project Board.

To use it in place of the Project Board, just don't make a Project Board. Put all the information—including the steps of all your projects and the approximate time you expect each to take—right on the Calendar.

It's up to you which way to go. Personally, I prefer using *both,* for one simple reason: I like being able to look at the wall and see the entire term at a glance. I find it much easier to see how everything fits together this way than by trying to "glance" at a dozen different weekly calendars or even three monthly ones.

I also find it difficult to see which steps go with which projects without studying the calendar (although I admit color-coding would solve the problem), whereas the very set-up of the Project Board makes such information easy to glean.

High school students may find it quite easy to use only the calendar, as they are usually not subject to quite as many long-term projects as college or graduate students. But once you're in college, especially if you have more than an average number of papers, reports, projects, etc., you'll find the Project Board a very helpful extra tool.

Planning your days and weeks

Now that you've got the "big picture"—the term—under control, it's time to learn about tools that will help you organize your days and weeks.

For any time management system to work, it has to be used continually. Make an appointment with yourself at the end of each week—Sunday night is perfect—to sit down and plan for the following week. This may just be the best time you spend all week, because you will reap the benefits of it throughout the week and beyond.

Step one: Make a "To Do" list

First, you must identify everything you need to do *this week*. Look at your Project Board and/or Term Planning Calendar to determine what tasks need to be completed this week for all your major school projects. Add any other tasks that must be done this week: from sending off a birthday present to your sister to attending your monthly volunteer meeting to completing homework that may have just been assigned.

Once you have created your list, you can move on to the next step, putting your tasks in order of importance.

Step two: Prioritize your tasks

When you sit down to study without a plan, you just dive into the first project that comes to mind. Of course, there's no guarantee that the first thing that comes to mind will be the most important. The point of the weekly

Priority Task Sheet is to help you arrange your tasks *in order of importance.* That way, even if you find yourself without enough time for everything, you can at least finish those assignments that are most important. A completed sample is on page 85; a blank form for you to photocopy is on page 98.)

First, ask yourself this question, "If I only got a few things done this week, what would I want them to be?" Mark these high-priority tasks with an "H." After you have identified the "urgent" items, consider those tasks that are *least* important—items which could wait until the following week to be done, if necessary. You may have tasks that you consider very important, but don't have to be completed this week. These items might be less important this week, but are likely to be rated higher next week. These are low-priority items; mark them with an "L."

All other items fit somewhere between the critical tasks and those of low priority. Review the remaining items, and if you're sure none of them are either "H" or "L," mark them with an "M" (for middle priority).

Step three: Fill in your Daily Schedule

Now you're ready to transfer the items on your Priority Task Sheet to your Daily Schedule forms. (See page 87 for a sample completed Schedule, page 99 for a form you can photocopy.)

Put in the "H" items first, followed by the "M" items. Then, fit in as many of the "L" items that you still have room for.

By following this procedure, you'll make sure you give the amount of time needed to your most important priorities. You can devote your most productive study times to your most important tasks, and plug in your lower priorities as they fit.

Priority Rating	Scheduled?	Priority Tasks This Week Week of 3/28 through 4/3
		Sociology Paper
H		– Library Search
M		– Outline
L		– Rough Draft
		Math Assignments
H		– Ch. 4
M		– Ch. 5
M		– study for test

Besides the importance of the task and the available time you have to complete it, other factors will determine how you fit your Daily Schedules together. Some will be beyond your control: work schedules, appointments with professors, counselors, doctors. But there are plenty of factors you *do* control, which you should consider as you put together your Daily Schedules for the week.

Schedule enough time for the task, but, particularly when working on long-term projects, not so much time that you "burn out." Every individual is different, but most students study best for blocks of about one and a half to three hours, depending on the subject. You might find history fascinating and be able to read for hours. Calculus, on the other hand, may be a subject that you can best handle in "small bites," a half-hour to an hour at a time.

Don't overdo it. Plan your study time in blocks, breaking up work time with short leisure activities. It's helpful to add these to your schedule as well. You'll find that these breaks help you think more clearly and creatively when you get back to studying.

Use your Daily Schedule *daily*

Each night (or in the morning before the day begins) look at your schedule for the upcoming day. How much free time is there? Are there "surprise" tasks that are not on your schedule but need to be? Are there conflicts you were not aware of at the beginning of the week? By checking your Daily Schedule *daily,* you'll be able to respond to these changes.

Using these tools effectively

There are thinkers and there are doers.
And there are those who think a lot about doing.

Daily Schedule

date: **3/30**

Assignments Due		Schedule
Bio. Lab work.	**5**	
Math, Ch. 4	**6**	
	7	
	8	
	9	Biology ↕
To Do/Errands	**10**	Sociology ↑
Call Erin – 871-4031	**11**	↓ ↓ ↓
Books to library	**12**	Lunch w/ Kim
☐ Bank	**1**	read:
☐ Groceries	**2**	ch.5 (50 c.) ↕
Drop by Jim's	**3**	Math class
	4	TRAVEL
	5	
Homework	**6**	Math homework ↑
1) Math Ch.5 1-9	**7**	work on paper ↓
2) Sociology paper	**8**	
(rough draft)	**9**	
	10	
	11	
	12	

Organizing your life requires you to actually *use* the Project Board, Term Planning Calendar, Priority Task Sheets and Daily Schedules. Once you have discovered habits and patterns of study that work for you, continue to use and hone them. Be flexible enough to add techniques you learn from others and alter schedules that circumstances have made obsolete.

Be realistic

Plan according to *your* schedule, *your* goals and *your* aptitudes, not some ephemeral "standard." Allocate the time you expect a project to take *you*, not the time it might take someone else, how long your teacher says it should take, etc. There will be tasks you accomplish far faster than anyone else, others that take you much longer.

Set priorities

Try to be realistic and honest with yourself when determining those things that require more effort, those that come easier to you. Refer back to the list of classes you like and dislike or do best and worst in. This will affect the time you need to allocate to specific projects.

Whenever possible, schedule pleasurable activities *after* study time, not before. They will then act as incentives, not distractions.

Be flexible

No calendar is an island. Any new assignment affects whatever you've already scheduled. If you have a reasonably light schedule when a new assignment suddenly appears, it can just be plugged right into your calendar and finished as scheduled. But if you've already scheduled virtually every hour for the next two weeks, *any* addition may force you to change a whole day's plan. Be flexible and be ready. It'll happen.

Monitor and adjust

No plan of action is foolproof, so monitor your progress at reasonable periods and make changes where necessary. Remember, this is *your* study regimen—you conceived it, you can change it. You may have allocated insufficient time to one assignment, too much to another. Fallen sick, gotten a little ahead and decided to run off for a ski weekend, received an unexpected assignment, etc.

I know you'll be anxious to stick to your schedule, to get things done. But taking a break and sitting back to survey the landscape of your efforts provides a good check and balance against costly mistakes and omissions. And don't forget to include the breaks you need, based on your answers in Chapter 1, in your allocation of study time.

Follow the scout motto

As assignments are entered on your calendar, make sure you also enter items needed—texts, other books you have to buy, borrow or get from the library, special materials (drawing pad, magic markers, graph paper, etc.).

Nothing's worse than sitting down to do that assignment you've put off for weeks...and realizing that though *you're* finally ready to get to work, your supplies *aren't*. Have your study materials available when you need them.

Everything's relative

Like time. Car trips take longer if you have to schedule frequent stops for gas, food, necessities, etc., longer still if you start one during rush hour. Likewise, libraries are more crowded at certain times of the day or year, which will affect how fast you can get books you need, etc. So take the time of day into account. And if your schedule involves working with others, take *their* sense of time into account. You may find you need to schedule "waiting time" for a chronically-late friend...and make sure you always have a book to read with you.

Try anything that works

You may decide that color coding your calendar—red for assignments that must be accomplished that week, blue for steps in longer-term assignments, yellow for personal time and appointments, green for classes, etc.— makes it easier for you to tell at a glance what you need to do and when you need to do it.

Once you've gotten used to your class schedule, you may decide to eliminate classes from your calendar and make it less complicated.

Adapt these tools to your own use. Try anything you think may work—use it if does, discard it if it doesn't.

One thing at a time

Accomplish one task before going on to the next one— don't skip around. If you ever stuffed envelopes for a political candidate, for example, you've probably already learned that it is far quicker and easier to sign 100 letters, then stuff them into envelopes, then seal and stamp them than to sign, stuff, seal and stamp one letter at a time.

Do your least favorite chores (study assignments, projects, whatever) first—you'll feel better having gotten them out of the way! And plan how to accomplish them as meticulously as possible. That will get rid of them even faster.

Pizza, anyone?

If you see that you are moving along faster than you anticipated on one task or project sequence, there is absolutely nothing wrong with continuing onto the next part of that assignment or the next project step. The alternative, of course, is to say *yea!*, forget the next assignment, finish early and buy a pizza.

And there's nothing wrong with the latter approach, either.

If you are behind, don't panic. Just take the time to reorganize your schedule and find the time you need to make up. You may be able to free up time from another task, put one part of a long-term project off for a day or two, etc. And if such rescheduling means cancelling a date or missing your favorite TV show, then it's up to you to decide which comes first.

Don't try to remember

All of the tools we've discussed and the various other hints, etc. should get you into the habit of writing things down. Amazingly you'll find that not having to remember all these items will free up space in your brain for the things you need to concentrate on or *do* have to remember. As a general rule, write down the so-called little things and you'll avoid data overload and clutter.

But don't forget!

As a time management axiom puts it, "Don't respond to the urgent and forget the important." It's easy to become distracted when the phone rings, your baby brother chooses to trash your room or you realize your favorite TV show is coming on. But don't just drop your books and run off. Take a few seconds to make sure you have reached a logical stopping point. If you haven't, get back to work. If you have, jot down a note to yourself of exactly where you left off and/or anything you want to remember after your break. Then you can enjoy your break without anxiety.

Don't do it twice

Some assignments—reading a novel, taking notes from a number of library books, etc.—can be interrupted at almost any time without causing a problem. Others may consist of a number of related steps, but you may still be able to pause after any step.

But beware of those time-consuming and complicated tasks that, once begun, demand to be completed. Taking notes from a number of books might be a task you can accomplish in half a dozen sittings, but reviewing and organizing them to outline your report definitely requires your undivided attention from start to finish. Interrupting at any point might mean starting all over again. What a waste of time *that* would be!

If you're writing and have a brainstorm—just as the phone rings (and you know it's from that person you've been waiting to hear from all week)—take a minute to at least jot down your ideas before you stop. Inspiration does not always drop in twice the same night. If you let yourself lose your "train of thought," you may find yourself alone at the station, watching your train chug off into the night.

Someone always knows better

Single out one or two fellow students—preferably with better grades—and compare notes. Not class notes, *study* notes—find out what's working for somebody else and try to incorporate these techniques into your own program.

Keep daydreams in their place

Nothing can be as counterproductive as losing your concentration, especially at critical times. Learn to ward off those enemies that would alter your course and you will find your journey much smoother.

Interruptions come in two distinct varieties: the unconscious and the conscious. The former include those distractions in your own mind that prevent clear and concentrated thinking—your fantasies and daydreams. Give in to these demons, lose your concentration, and you will find hours happily drifting by. Unfortunately, when you get to the end of the day, you will find you have accomplished nothing on your list. Trust me: The depression from falling behind will not be assuaged by the glow of your fantasies!

Know your study clock

One way to guard against these mental intrusions is to know your own study clock and plan your study time accordingly. Each of us is predisposed to function most efficiently at specific times of the day (or night). Find out what sort of study clock you are on and schedule your work during this period. (Most people's peak activity hours fall during the mid-day period. There is a notable reduction of productive hours starting with late afternoon.)

This is not a foolproof solution, however. Even if you're always on schedule, have every material you need and organized your calendar with more colors than a box of Crayolas, you may find yourself staring out the window and dreaming of (choose one) a boy, a girl, a night, a weekend, a trip, an adventure, a TV show, a fantasy, or just the way the sun reflects in the pond. Life is like that.

So what do you do?

(1) Banish those thoughts as fast and furiously as Salem handled witches. Shorten the scheduled time before your next break and, when you take that break, enjoy it! Then go back to work. If it continues happening, take more frequent breaks or just keep plugging away. Like anything else, concentration is a learned skill, one in which practice *does* make perfect.

(2) Say the heck with it and take a break right away. If your schedule is loose enough, give yourself an hour, the morning or even the rest of the day off. Fantasize to your heart's content (or, even better, go out and *do* something about the fantasies), then go back to studying with a mind ready to concentrate on the task at hand.

Neither one of these solutions is always right. There are times to fight the dreams and there are days to say the heck with it and go to a ball game.

Noids to avoid

The second category of intrusions are conscious acts or activities. Beware of uninvited guests and *all* phone calls: Unless you are ready to take a break, they will only get you off schedule.

More subtle enemies include the sudden desire to sharpen every pencil in the house, an unheard-of urge to clean your room, an offer to do your sister's homework. Anything, in other words, to avoid your own work. If you find yourself doing anything *but* your work, either take a break then and there or pull yourself together and get down to work. Self-discipline, too, is a learned habit that gets easier with practice.

The simple act of saying "no!" (to others or to yourself) will help insulate yourself from these unnecessary (and certainly postponable) interruptions. Remember, what you are seeking to achieve is not just time—but *quality* time. Put your "do not disturb" sign up and stick to your guns, no matter what the temptation.

Reward yourself

In line with my advice above, there *are* times to ignore the schedule, pat yourself on the back and take off and lie on the grass. But why wait until the siren call of interruption forces you to waste precious time fighting for concentration—especially if you wind up just giving in anyway? Why not incorporate "reward time" into your regular schedule?

Depending on your schedule, of course, this could mean a night off every week to do something you like, a weekend a month, etc. Alternatively, each day (if you really need help, each *hour*) you could simply set up a reward as an incentive for finishing an assignment, a project, a day's work, whatever.

Rewards do not necessarily require large amounts of cash, long trips or other people. The more frequently you run into trouble concentrating on the task at hand, the more frequently you should create some incentive to help yourself: "If I get this next thing done, I'll take off 15 minutes and have an ice cream." Then enjoy the whole banana split!

Now comes the payoff

Once you start using your Project Board, Term Planning Calendar, Priority Task Sheets and Daily Schedules, you will reap the benefits every day.

Anything—even school—seems less overwhelming when you have it broken into "bite-size" pieces...and you already know the flavor.

You no longer worry about when you'll get that paper done—you've already planned for it.

You'll accomplish it all—one step at a time.

My time management program allows for flexibility. In fact, I encourage you to adapt any of my recommendations to your own unique needs. That means it will work for you whether you are living in a dorm, sharing an apartment or house with roommates, or living with a spouse and children. That you *can* learn how to balance school, work, fun, and even family obligations.

As you get used to managing your time, planning ahead as well as planning your week and even your days, you'll quickly discover that you seem to have more time than ever before.

(Please feel free to photocopy the blank forms on pp. 97 - 99 and use them in your own time management system.)

Term Planning Calendar

Fill in due dates for assignments and papers, dates of tests, and important non-academic activities and events

Month	Mon	Tue	Wed	Thu	Fri	Sat	Sun

Priority Rating	Scheduled?	Priority Tasks This Week
		Week of _____ through _____

Daily Schedule

date: _____

Assignments Due

To Do/Errands

Homework

Schedule

Time	
5	
6	
7	
8	
9	
10	
11	
12	
1	
2	
3	
4	
5	
6	
7	
8	
9	
10	
11	
12	

Chapter 5

HOW TO
Excel
In
Class

Whatever your grade level, whatever your grades, whatever your major, whatever your ultimate career goals, you (and I) all have one thing in common: the classroom experience.

Most teachers utilize the classroom setting as an opportunity to embellish and interpret material covered in the text and other assigned readings. If you always complete your reading assignments before class, you'll be able to devote your classroom time to the "add-on" angles the teacher will undoubtedly cover.

Exactly how you'll use the skills we'll cover in this chapter will be influenced by two factors: the type of classroom set up and the particular methods and styles employed by each of your teachers.

Each of the following general class formats will require adjustments to accomplish the above goals:

Lectures: Podium pleasantries

Teacher speaks, students listen. Lectures are quite common from the college level up, but exist only rarely at the high school level. Lecture halls at larger colleges may fill up with hundreds of students for some of the more popular courses.

Primary Emphases: Listening; note taking.

Discussions: Time to speak your mind

Also called *tutorials* or *seminars,* discussion groups are again common on the college level, often as adjuncts to courses boasting particularly large enrollments. A typical weekly schedule for such a course might consist of two lectures and one or more discussion groups. Often led by graduate teaching assistants, these discussion groups are much smaller—usually no larger than two dozen students—and give you the chance to discuss points made in the lecture and material from the text and other assigned reading.

Primary Emphases: Asking/answering questions; analyzing concepts and ideas; taking part in discussion.

Such groups rarely follow a precise text or format and may wander wildly from topic to topic, once again pointing out the need for a general mastery of the course material, the "jumping off" point for discussion.

Combination: Best (or worst) of both

And some post-secondary courses are, for want of a better term, ***Combination Classes***; that is, they combine the lecture and discussion formats. The teacher prepares a lesson plan of material he or she wants covered in a specific class. Through lecture, discussion, question and answer, audio-visual presentations or a combination of one or more such devices, the material is covered.

Your preparation for this type of class will depend to a great extent on the approach of each individual instructor. Such classes also occur on the post-secondary level—college, graduate school, trade school—when class size is too small for a formal lecture approach.

Primary Emphases: Note taking; listening; participation; asking and answering questions.

Hands-on: Getting your hands dirty

Hands-on classes, including science labs and various vocational education courses (industrial arts, graphics, etc.), occur at all levels, from high school up.

They are concerned almost exclusively with *doing* something—completing a particular experiment, working on a project, etc. The teacher may demonstrate certain things before letting the students work on their own, but the primary emphasis is on the student carrying out his or her own projects while in class.

On the college level, science labs are merely overseen by graduate assistants. Trade schools may use a combination of short lectures and demonstrations and hands-on workshops—you can't become a good auto mechanic just by reading a book on cleaning a distributor.

Primary Emphasis: Development and application of particular manual and technical skills

Rarely can a single class be neatly pigeonholed into one of these formats, though virtually all will be primarily one or another. It would seem that size is a key factor in choosing a format, but you can't always assume, for example, that a large lecture course, filled with 200 or more students, will feature a professor standing behind a rostrum reading from his prepared text. Or that a small class of a dozen people will tend to be all discussion.

During my college years, for example, I had a Religion teacher who, though his class was one of the more popular on campus and regularly drew 300 or more students to each session, rarely lectured at all. One never knew *what* to expect when entering his classroom. One week it would be a series of musical improvisations from a local jazz band, with a variety of graduate assistants talking about out-of-body (religious, note the tie-in) experiences. Another session would consist entirely of the professor arguing with a single student over one key topic... which had *nothing* to do with that week's (or any *other* week's) assignment.

In another class of merely 20 students, the professor teaching us Physical Chemistry would march in at the sound of the bell and, without acknowledging anyone's presence or saying a word, walk to the blackboard and start writing equations, which he would continue to do, working his way across the massive board, until, some 20 or 30 minutes later, he ran off the right side. Slowly, he would walk back to the left side...and start writing all over again. He never asked questions. Never asked *for* questions. In fact, I'm not sure I remember him uttering *any*thing for three solid months!

Know your teacher

What is also extremely important for you to know and understand is the kind of teacher you've got and his or her likes, dislikes, preferences, style and what he or she expects you to get out of his or her class. Depending on your analysis of your teacher's habits, goals and tendencies, preparation may vary quite a bit, whatever the chosen format.

Some teachers are very confident fielding questions at any point during a lesson; others prefer questions to be held until the end of the day's lesson; still others, and my chemistry prof. is a good example, discourage questions (or any interaction for that matter) entirely. Learn when and how your teacher likes to field questions and ask them accordingly.

No matter how ready a class is to enter into a freewheeling discussion, some teachers fear losing control and veering away from their very specific lesson plan. Such teachers may well encourage discussion but always try to steer it into the set path they've decided upon. Other teachers thrive on chaos, in which case you can never be sure just what's going to happen.

Approaching a class with the former teacher should lead you to participate as much as possible in the class discussion, but warn you to stay within whatever boundaries he or she has obviously set.

Getting ready for a class taught by the latter kind of teacher requires much more than just reading the text—there will be a lot of emphasis on your understanding key concepts, interpretation, analysis and your ability to apply those lessons to cases never mentioned in your text at all!

Some teachers' lesson plans or lectures are, at worst, merely a review of what's in the text or, at best, a review plus some discussion of sticky points or areas he or she feels may give you problems. Others use the text or other assignments merely as a jumping off point—their lectures or lesson plans might cover numerous points that aren't in your text at all. Preparing for the latter kind of class will require much more than rote memorization of facts and figures—you'll have to be ready to give examples, explain concepts in context and more.

Most of your teachers and professors will probably have the same goals: to teach you how to think, learn important facts and principles of the specific subject they teach and, perhaps, how to apply them in your own way.

In classes like math or science, your ability to apply what you've learned to specific problems is paramount.

Others, like your English teacher, will require you to analyze and interpret various works, but may emphasize the "correct" interpretation, too.

Whatever situation you find yourself in—and you may well have one or more of each of the above "types"—you will need to adapt the skills we will cover in this chapter to each situation.

In general, here's how you should plan to prepare for any class before you walk through the door and take your seat:

Complete all assignments

Regardless of a particular teacher's style or the classroom format he or she is using, virtually every course you take will have a formal text (or two or three or more) assigned to it. Though the way the text explains or covers particular topics may differ substantially from your teacher's approach to the same material, your text is still the basis of the course and a key ingredient in your studying. You *must* read it, plus any other assigned books, *before* you get to class.

You may sometimes feel you can get away without reading assigned books beforehand, especially in a lecture format where you *know* the chance of being called on is slim to none. But fear of being questioned on the material is certainly not the only reason I stress reading the material that's been assigned. You will be lost if the professor decides—for the first time ever!—to spend the entire period asking *the students* questions. I've had it happen. And it was *not* a pleasant experience for the unprepared.

You'll also find it harder to take clear and concise notes because you won't know what's in the text, in which case you'll be frantically taking notes on material you'd be underlining in your books, or be able to evaluate important vs. unimportant information.

If you're heading for a discussion group, how can you participate without your reading as a basis? I think the lousiest feeling in the world is sitting in a classroom knowing that, sooner or later, you are going to be called on and that you don't know the material.

Remember: This includes not just reading the main text but any other books, articles, etc. previously assigned, plus handouts that may have been previously passed out. It also means completing any non-reading assignments— having a paper topic ready, preparing a list of topics, etc.

Review your notes

Both from your reading and from the previous class. Your teacher is probably going to start this lecture or discussion from the point he or she left off last time. And you probably won't remember where that point was from week to week...unless you check your notes.

Have questions ready

As discussed in Chapter 3, preparing questions as you read text material is an important step. Here's your chance to find the answers to the questions that are still puzzling you. Go over your questions before class. That way, you'll be able to check off the ones the lecturer or teacher answers along the way and only ask those left unanswered.

Prepare required materials

Including your notebook, text, pens or pencils and other such basics, plus particular class requirements like a calculator, drawing paper, other books, etc.

Before we get into how to take notes, it's important to talk about how to set up your notebook(s). There are a variety of ways you can organize your note-taking system:

1. Get one big two- or three-ring binder (probably three or more inches thick) that will be used for all notes from all classes. This will require a hole punch, "tab" dividers and a healthy supply of pre-punched paper.

   You can divide the binder into separate sections for each course/class, in each of which you will keep notes from your lectures and discussion groups, reading lists, assignment deadlines and any course handouts, all material set up in chronological fashion. Alternatively, you can further subdivide each section into separate sections for reading notes, class notes and handouts.

2. Use one of the above systems but get smaller binders, one for each course/class.

3. Use separate notebooks (they're a lot lighter than binders) for notes, both from your reading and class. Use file folders for each class to keep handouts, project notes and copies, etc. They can be kept in an accordion file or in a multi-pocketed folder.

Whichever system you choose—one of the above or an ingenious one of your own—do *not* use the note card system for preparing papers and oral reports you will learn in chapter 7. While it's my all-time favorite system for that application, it does *not* work well for class note taking...and I've tried it.

Prepare your attitude

And don't discount the importance of the way you approach each class mentally—getting the most out of school in general and any class in particular depends in good measure on how ready you are to really take part in the process. You must be "up" for school, "up" for each class. It is *not* sufficient, even if you're otherwise well-prepared, to just sit back and absorb the information. Learning requires your active participation every step of the way.

What to do in class

Keep in mind your own preferences and under what circumstances you do best—refer back to the first two chapters and review your skills lists. You'll need to concentrate hardest on those courses in which you do most poorly, no matter what the style of the teacher.

Sit near the front. You should make distraction as difficult as possible by sitting as close to the instructor as you can.

You've probably realized by now that the farther you sit from the teacher, the more difficult it is to listen. Sitting toward the back of the room means more heads bobbing around in front of you, more students staring out the window...and encouraging you to do the same.

Sitting up front has several benefits.

You will make a terrific first impression on the instructor since you might very well be the only student taking a seat in the front row. He'll see immediately that you have come to class to listen and learn, not just take up space.

You'll be able to hear the instructor's voice clearly, and the instructor will be able to hear *you* clearly when you ask and answer questions.

Finally, being able to see the teacher clearly will help ensure that your eyes don't wander around the room and out the windows, taking your brain with them.

So, if you have the option of picking your desk in class, do as they say in the old spiritual: Sit right down front.

Avoid distracting classmates. The gum cracker. The doodler. The practical jokester. The whisperer. Even the perfume sprayer. Your fellow classmates may be kind and thoughtful friends, entertaining lunch companions and great fun at parties, but their little quirks, idiosyncrasies and personal hygiene habits can prove distracting when you sit next to them in class. Knuckle-cracking and note-passing are just some of the evils that can divert your attention in the middle of your biology professor's discourse on bivalves. Avoid them.

Sit up straight. Do I sound like your mother? I know you don't want to hear it, but for once she's right. To listen effectively, you must sit correctly, in a way that will let you stay comfortable and relatively still during the entire lecture. If parts of your body start to ache or fall asleep, your attention will inevitably wander. "The mind can retain only as much as the bottom can sustain."

Look for nonverbal clues

Studies have shown that only a fraction of communications is carried in the words themselves. A great deal of the message we receive when someone is speaking to us comes from body language, facial expression and tone of voice.

Most instructors will go off on tangents of varying relevance to the subject matter. Some of these will be important, but, at least during your first few lessons with that particular teacher, you won't know which.

Body language can be your clue.

If the teacher begins looking at the window or his eyes glaze over, he's sending you a clear signal: "Put your pen down. This isn't going to be on any test."

On the other hand, if he turns to write something down on the blackboard, makes eye contact with several students and/or gestures dramatically, he's sending an even clearer signal about the importance of the point he's making.

Of course, there are exceptions to this rule. There was a trigonometry professor I endured who would get most worked up about the damage being done to the nation's sidewalks by the deadly menace of chewing gum.

Ask questions

No, don't raise your hand to ask or answer questions every 90 seconds. Being an active listener means asking *yourself* if you understand everything that has been discussed. If the answer is "no," ask the instructor questions at an appropriate time or write down questions that you must have answered to understand the subject fully.

Challenge yourself to draw conclusions from the things that the instructor is saying. Don't just sit there letting your hand take notes. Let your mind do something, too. Think about the subject matter, how it relates to what you've been assigned to read and other facts you've been exposed to.

To tape or not to tape

I am opposed to using a tape recorder as a substitute for an active brain in class for the following reasons:

- *It is time-consuming.* To be cynical about it, not only will you have to waste time sitting in class, you'll have to waste more time listening to that class *again!*

- *It is virtually useless for review.* Rewinding and fast-forwarding through cassettes to find the salient points of a lecture can be torture. During the hectic days before an exam, are you going to want to waste time listening to a lecture when you can read so much more quickly?

- *It offers no back-up.* Only the most diligent students will record *and* take notes. What happens if your tape recorder malfunctions? How useful will blank or distorted tapes be when it's time to review? If you're going to take notes as a back-up, why not just do a good job note-taking and save the time and effort of listening to that lecture again?

- *It costs money.* Compare the price of blank paper and a pen to that of a recorder, batteries and tapes. The cost of batteries *alone* should convince you that you're better off going the low-tech route. (Save those batteries for your Walkman.)

- When you rely on your tape-recorded lecture for garnering notes, *you miss those "live" clues* we discussed earlier. When all you have is a tape of your lecture, you don't see

that zealous flash in your teacher's eyes, the
passionate arm-flailing, the stern set of the
jaw, all of which should scream, "Listen up.
This will be on your test!"

Having said all this against tape recorders and note-
taking, I concede that there are situations in which tape
recorders can be useful—such as when your head is so
stuffed up with a cold that "active listening" during an
hour-long lecture is virtually impossible. With this
exception noted, I still maintain that a tape recorder is no
substitute for good listening skills.

Taking notes

Taking concise, clear notes is first and foremost the
practice of discrimination—developing your ability to
separate the essential from the superfluous, the key
concepts, key facts, key ideas from all the rest. In turn,
this requires the ability to listen to what your teacher is
saying and copying down only what you need to in order to
understand the concept. For some, that could mean a
single sentence. For others, a detailed example will be the
key.

Just remember: The quality of your notes usually has
little to do with their *length*—three key lines that reveal
the core concepts of a whole lecture are far more valuable
than paragraphs of less important data.

Understand the big picture

If you are actively listening, and listening before you
write, then your understanding of the "big picture" ought
to follow naturally. Let's say your history teacher is
rattling off dates and names of battles. Your note-passing
classmate in the back may go into a panic as he scrambles

to jot down all the tongue-twisting foreign names that she's shooting off faster than a machine gun.

But *you*, who are sitting up front and listening actively, pause with pen in hand as your teacher sums up her point: that battle activity increased to a frenzy in the final months before the war's end. You jot down a brief note to that effect, knowing that you can check your textbook for all the names, dates and details of specific battles.

Your poor friend in the back, while capturing most of the battle names, missed the main point, the big picture, and now will feel compelled to memorize the list of names and dates, even though he doesn't know why he copied them down in the first place.

Take notes on what you *don't* know

You *know* the first line of the Gettysburg address. You know the formula for Einstein's theory of relativity. You know what date Pearl Harbor was bombed. So why waste time and space writing them down?

Frequently, your teacher presents material that is commonly known in order to set the stage for further discussion, or to introduce material that is more difficult. Don't be so conditioned to write down dates, vocabulary, terms and names that you mindlessly scribble down information you already know.

Tailor your note-taking to class format

The extent of note-taking required—as well as the importance of those notes to your success in class—will depend largely on the format of the class. In a lecture, for example, your teacher might not even know your name. Consequently, your note-taking and listening skills are all you will have in your quest for top grades.

Seminars or discussion groups place a great deal of emphasis on your question-asking and answering skills. But you should not neglect taking notes. Be all ears while the discussion is flowing, but, as soon as possible after class, write down the most important points discussed.

In hands-on classes, such as science and language labs, art classes and courses in industrial skills, keep a notebook handy in case something comes up that you think you should remember for an exam. I had a chemistry teacher who, during labs, quite often launched into extensive discussions on theory. The less dull-witted among us quickly learned to keep our notebooks close by, capturing facts and figures he never mentioned in class ...but did on the exams!

Develop your shorthand skills

You don't have to be a master of shorthand to utilize helpful abbreviations for note-taking. Leaving out the unnecessary vowels and articles is just one of the tricks to writing quickly while you are taking notes. You can mentally insert them while you're reading your notes over, so why write them when you're struggling to get on paper all of the really *important* things your instructor is saying?

Here is a list of standard abbreviations that will help you out in most of your classes (you may recognize many of these symbols from math and logic):

$\approx$	*Approximately*
w/	*With*
w/o	*Without*
wh/	*Which*
$\rightarrow$	*Resulting in*

←	*As a result of/consequence of*
+	*And or also*
*	*Most importantly*
ff	*Following*
<	*Less than*
>	*More than*
=	*The same as, equal to*
↑	*Increasing*
↓	*Decreasing*
esp	*Especially*
Δ	*Change*
∴	*Therefore*

Expanding on your "shorthand"

While you're listening to your instructor, you should be thinking about what you write down. Lectures are filled with so many words that will not be at all helpful when you sit down to study for the big exam. Writing *those* words down and missing some of the truly important points of the lecture is counterproductive: Your notes may look impressively complete, but what are they completely full of? All the important stuff, or...?

For instance, if your teacher says, "The harsh terms of the Treaty of Versailles and the ineffectiveness of the Weimar Republic were two of the most prevalent themes in the early speeches of Hitler," you could write down something like:

Erly Hitler speeches: *hrsh Versailles Trty, Wmr wknss.

If the Treaty of Versailles is something that has been discussed frequently in class, you might just write "Vrs." Continue to abbreviate *more* as more terms become readily recognizable—in that way, the speed and effectiveness of your note-taking will increase as the school year grinds on.

I've also noticed that many students are prone to write *big* when they are writing fast and to use only a portion of the width of their paper. I guess they figure that turning over pages quickly means they are taking great notes. All it really means is that they are taking notes that will be difficult to read or use when it's review time. Force yourself to write small and take advantage of the entire width of your note paper.

Now, let's look at a sample lecture so you can practice your newly developed skills. I hope you like comparative literature!

Hitting all the right notes

Here is part of a lecture that was one of my favorites in college. It is about the comic novel. I've numbered the paragraphs here so that they can be referred to easily later on.

The Comic Perspective
In Comic Novels

1   The comic perspective is one which finds its most successful expression in a presentation of contrasting methods of viewing the world. These could be categorized as that of the cynic and that of the saint. The laughter and the sense of irony that a comic work of literature can instill in its readers is a result of the clash between these methods of seeing the world.

2   If the work of literature is to be considered at all successful, its readers will surely find themselves beset with the task of sorting among the alternatives offered by the idealistic and realistic sensibilities embodied within the characters and/or the narrative voice.

3   The comic novel is one which, at last, must leave its readers experiencing its world in the way a child experiences his: with wonder, honesty, imagination and confusion.

4   If we conduct an overview of protagonists in great comic novels, we find characters who are very much like children. They are innocent, idealistic and often naive. Moreover, authors of the great comic novels go to great lengths to deny their characters a detailed past. It is almost as if the protagonists are born fully grown into the world of the novel.

5   We can learn very few biographical details about Don Quixote. We are told only that he has filled his head with the ideals and dreams of chivalry through his incessant reading of romantic literature. Moving ahead to Dickens, we find in The Pickwick Papers a protagonist that the author continually denies a past. It is as if, for Dickens, the intrusion or even the introduction of the past into the present must inevitably bring with it a diminution of integrity and self-sufficiency. In fact, the only instance of Mr. Pickwick attempting to remember his past results in the protagonist falling asleep before he can do so.

6   When we get to the 20th-century comic novels we notice a continuity of this device. Paul Pennyfeather is delivered into the chaotic world of Decline and Fall as if from a womb. Evelyn Waugh devotes three sentences to the history of his protagonist. He is an orphan (someone who by definition cannot know his past) who "lived in Onslow Square with his guardian, who was abysmally bored by his company..."

While you don't have the luxury of being able to *hear* these words, as, of course, you would in a real lecture, pretend that you were suddenly stripped of the benefits afforded by the printed page—the ability to reread a portion of a lecture that you wouldn't be able to "rehear."

What would you come up with? How many of the actual words from the lecture would turn up in your notes? Would you be trying to get down everything the professor said?

While this lecture *sounds* eloquent, it has more sizzle to it than steak. Hence, your notes can be quite brief. Here are what mine looked like (with the paragraph references added):

Cmc Prspctv in Cmc Nvls

1. CP=2 wys seeing wrld—cynic, saint. Clash=lftr
2. Chrctrs, nrrtr embdy idlsm or rlsm
3. Rdr xprnc=chld's wrld view=cnfused, inncnt
4. Prtgnsts like chldrn—no past
5. e.g. Dkns/Pkwk, Cvnts/DonQ
6. e.g. Wgh/Pnnyftr

It isn't pretty, but it works

Trying to capture the eloquence and missing half of the teacher's points would make much less sense.

What taking such brief notes will do is allow you to sit back, listen, and watch the instructor. This will help you capture the entire *message* that he or she is communicating, not just the *words*. If you think that the words are very important, try to elaborate on your shorthand while the professor's words are still rattling around in your head—right after the lecture. It's not a bad idea to do this anyway, especially as you start to develop your own note-taking shorthand. It'll allow you to make sure you understand your own abbreviations.

But is it good for you?

Do you think this sort of shorthand will work for you? You probably won't at first. When I worked as a reporter, I found that I couldn't trust my notes, at least not in the beginning. But in trying to write so much down I also discovered that I couldn't trust my note-*taking*. As I gained more experience, my note-taking became more and more productive.

Just be careful—in your fervor to adopt my shorthand system, don't abbreviate so much that your notes are absolutely unintelligible to you almost as soon as you write them!

The point here is, you must come up with a note-taking shorthand system that makes sense to *you*. You may certainly choose to abbreviate less, to write a little more. Whatever system you develop, just make sure it serves the same purpose: giving you the time to really *listen* to your instructors, rather than writing down only what they say.

Participating

In many non-lecture classes, you will find that discussion, mostly in the form of questions and answers, is actively encouraged. This dialogue serves to both confirm your knowledge and comprehension of specific subject matter and identify those areas in which you need work.

Whatever the format in which you find yourself, participate in any discussion to the best of your ability. Most teachers consider class participation a key ingredient in the grades they mete out. No matter how many papers and tests you ace, if you never open your mouth in class, you may be surprised (but shouldn't be) to get less than an "A."

If you are having trouble following a particular line of thought or argument, ask for a review or for clarification.

Don't ask questions or make points looking to impress your teacher—your real motive will probably be pretty obvious. Remember what you *are* there for—to learn the material and master it.

Based on the professor's preferences and the class set up, ask the questions you feel need answers.

Finally, listen closely to the words of your classmates. Knowledge has no boundaries, and you'll often find their comments, attitudes and opinions as helpful and insightful as your instructor's.

What if you're shy or just get numb whenever you're called on? Ask a question rather than taking part in the discussion—it's easier and, over time, may help you break the ice and jump into the discussion. If you really can't open your mouth without running a fever, consider a remedial course, like Dale Carnegie.

Most importantly, prepare and practice. Fear of standing in front of a class or even of participating from the safety of your seat is, for many of you, really a symptom of lack of confidence.

And *lack of confidence stems from lack of preparation.* The more prepared you are—if you know the material backwards and forwards—the more likely you will be able, even *want,* to raise your hand and "strut your stuff." Practicing with friends, parents or relatives may also help.

If you are having trouble with oral reports, they are covered separately in chapter 7. I think you'll find the hints I've included there will eliminate a lot of the fear such talks seem to engender.

What to do *after* class

As soon as possible after your class, review your notes, fill in the "blanks," mark down questions you need to research in your text or ask during the next class, and remember to mark any new assignments on your weekly calendar.

I tend to discourage recopying your notes as a general practice, since I believe it's more important to work on taking good notes the first time around and not wasting the time it takes to recopy. *But* if you tend to write fast and illegibly, it might also be a good time to rewrite your notes so they're readable, taking the opportunity to summarize as you go. The better your notes, the better your chance of capturing and recalling the pertinent material.

It is not easy for most high school students to do so, but in college, where you have a greater say in scheduling your classes, this is why I recommend "one period on, one off"—an open period, even a half hour, after each class to review that class's notes and prepare for the next one.

Chapter 6

HOW TO
Use
Your
Library

Libraries contain the written record of Humankind's brief stay on Planet Earth. They stand unparalleled as one of our finest accomplishments and unchallenged as a reference and research source. In your attempt to develop lifelong study skills, you will find yourself using this resource constantly. The library presents a single well from which we can draw knowledge and material throughout our lifetimes...without ever worrying about coming up dry.

Libraries are a staple in cities large and small across the country and represent an amazingly democratic aspect of our culture. Rules and restrictions vary from library to library—public vs. college, large vs. small—but high school and college students usually have access to virtually all library materials. And remember: These services are *free*. A library card is your ticket to the world of knowledge that could keep you busy for the rest of your life.

Where to find a library

Start with your local phone directory. I can virtually guarantee there is a library within minutes of your home, since according to the two volumes of the 41st edition of *The American Library Directory* (R.R. Bowker, New York, NY), there are 15,013 public and 4,647 academic (high school, college, university and graduate school) libraries in the United States. These are the ones you would most likely be using. (Naturally, you'll find these volumes, with listings of all U.S. libraries by state and city, in your library.)

If for some reason you don't think the resources of these nearly 20,000 libraries are sufficient, there are also nearly 500 libraries on military bases throughout the country, plus over 10,000 government and special (law, medical, religious, art, etc.) libraries nationwide.

Many major university libraries dwarf all but the largest public library systems. Harvard, at more than eight million volumes the largest university library in the country, Yale, Princeton and similar bastions of learning offer tremendous resources even the major public libraries can't. If you have access to a major university library, consider it your good fortune and take advantage of it.

How libraries work

Most libraries are divided into reading rooms, restricted collections and unrestricted book stacks. Unrestricted book stacks are those through which anyone using the library can wander, choosing books to use while in the library or, if allowed, to take home. Restricted areas generally include any special collections of rare books, those open only to scholars or to those with particular credentials, either by library rule or by order of whoever donated the collection (and, often, the room housing it) to the library. In some libraries, *all* book stacks are closed, and *all* books must be obtained from a librarian.

Most libraries contain both *circulating materials*— those books and other items you may check out and take home with you— and *non-circulating material*—those that must be used only in the library. All fiction, general non-fiction and even most "scholarly" titles will usually be found in the first group. Reference material, periodicals and books in special collections are usually in the second.

A look at a major library

How extensive is the collection of information at a major institution like the New York Public Library?

You'd be amazed.

Let's look only at the main library on Fifth Avenue, which stands like a monument at the dividing line between the East and West sides of Manhattan.

The first thing you discover is that no books can be taken out of this building. Since there are 82 branches throughout the five boroughs of New York (which together house over 13,000,000 volumes) that *will* let you take out many of their holdings, this is not exactly a problem.

So you can't take anything with you. What can you study while you're there? In addition to an extensive collection of the fiction and non-fiction works you'd expect to find in such a library, shelves of books on every conceivable topic from Airplanes to Zoology, back issues of more periodicals than you could probably name and more recordings than your local record store stocks, there are separate rooms—that's right, *rooms* (and large ones, too!)—for prints and photographs, art, microfilm, U.S. and local history and genealogy, rare books, manuscripts, archives, maps, a Science and Technology Research Center, Economic and Public Affairs Center, Slavonic and Oriental Divisions. (In the system as a whole there's also an extensive Afro-American collection and a separate Library for the Blind and Physically Handicapped.) While a few of the more specialized collections (rare books, manuscripts, prints and photographs) require a special card just to enter the collection, most of the rest of this amazing storehouse of knowledge is open to the public!

But the NYPL also demonstrates through its many programs that the library is much more than just a repository for books. It offers a daily program of films, lectures, book discussion groups, plays, poetry readings, concerts and exhibits for adults, films, story telling and pre-school programs for children, and is a meeting place for a wide variety of community, consumer, educational, health, social service, religious and cultural groups.

You could live at the NYPL and *never* get bored!

What about *your* library?

What? You don't live in New York? And you doubt your local library can compete?

You'd be surprised at how wrong you probably are. I live in Hawthorne, New Jersey, a small suburban community. My local library—the Louis Bay IInd Library, officially—is probably typical of the kind of library you'll be working in. So a look at my library should help you appreciate what you can do at yours.

Its collection includes more than 70,000 books, current and back issues of nearly 200 magazines and newspapers, plus a variety of other material: microfiche, microfilm, compact discs, audio cassettes, phonograph records, videotapes, plus children's books and audio tapes, film-strips and videocassettes. Not unimpressive, but a mere *one two-hundredth* of the collection available at the NYPL.

Ah, but remember the wonders the computer hath wrought. Through a worksharing program with the library of Fair Lawn, the community next door, you can sit in the Hawthorne library and search on-line through Fair Lawn's collection of books—another 150,000 volumes. And if you need other periodicals, you have computer access to a list of the 1,500 titles in the nearby Fairleigh Dickinson University library, any of which you can obtain by FAX in minutes.

You can sit at a computer terminal in Hawthorne and access the more than six million volumes at Princeton University's Firestone Library, the second largest library in the New York Metropolitan area (after the New York Public Library) and larger than any other public library in the nation (except for the gargantuan Library of Congress, which is a special case).

Right now, by networking with other libraries, my Hawthorne librarian could track down virtually any book, magazine, newspaper, phonograph record, audio or video cassette you want if given a reasonable amount of time.

And networking is the word of the future. In New Jersey, for example, many of the counties have already tied together all the individual libraries within their bor-ders. In the near future, every county in New Jersey will have a county-wide library networking system in place. One to two years after that, every library in the *state* will be tied together by connecting all the county systems.

Don't be surprised if within our lifetimes—and I left Teenland some years ago—even the smallest libraries will boast computer terminals that will enable you to call up any book or periodical in any other library...in the world.

How to use your library

So as to provide organization and facilitate access, most libraries utilize the Dewey Decimal Classification System, which uses numbers from 000 to 999 to classify all material by subject matter. It begins by organizing all books into ten major groupings:

000 - 099	General
100 - 199	Philosophy
200 - 299	Religion
300 - 399	Social Sciences
400 - 499	Language
500 - 599	Science
600 - 699	Useful Arts
700 - 799	Fine Arts
800 - 899	Literature
900 - 999	History

Given the millions of books available in major libraries, just dividing them into these 10 groups would still make it quite difficult to find a specific title. So each of the 10 major groupings is further divided into 10 and each of these now one hundred groups is assigned to more specific subjects within each large group. For example, within the Philosophy classification (100), 150 is psychology and 170 is ethics. Within the history classification (900), 910 is travel and 930 is ancient history.

There is even further subdivision. Mathematics is given its own number in the 500 (Science) series—510. But specific subjects within mathematics are further classified: 511 is arithmetic; 512, algebra, and so on.

Finally, to simplify your task even more, the last two digits in the Dewey code signify the type of book:

01   Philosophy of
02   Outlines of
03   Dictionary of
04   Essays about
05   Periodicals on
06   Society transactions and proceedings
07   Study or teaching of
08   Collections
09   History of

There are more than 50,000 new books published each year, and your library probably buys a number of these. Books arrive almost daily and are sent to the cataloging section for classification, special bindings (if needed) and shelf placement. Once entered into the system, books are indexed in the card catalog by author, title and subject matter. Finding a biography of Tolstoy, for example, is as easy as looking up Tolstoy in the card catalog and copying down the appropriate codes for the particular one you want (yes, your library probably has more than one!).

In a closed-shelf environment, you would give the appropriate numbers to a librarian and the books would be delivered to you. If the shelves are open, you have merely to learn the way they are organized and go search after your own books. Open shelf areas are often designated by letters of the alphabet (for fiction), by subject matter (in smaller libraries), or, in virtually all major libraries, according to the Dewey classification code.

You may go to your local library and not even find a card catalog, which might confuse you. Am I out of touch? Hopelessly antiquated? Computers are taking over the world of business, so it's no surprise that a recordintensive "business" like the library is in the forefront of computerization. Librarians I've spoken to estimate that by the year 2000—less than a decade from now—95 percent of all U.S. libraries will be "on line"—with "user friendly" computer terminals replacing old fashioned catalog cards. Roughly 40 percent of all libraries—maybe yours— already *are* on line.

Computers also mean more things you can do. For example, at the New York Public Library there are Apple microcomputers offering more than 100 programs, from practice math problems to SAT preparation and, of course, computer games, at more than 30 locations.

Where to start

Still feeling overwhelmed by the stacks of volumes, Dewey Decimal system, card catalogs and computers? You still have no excuse for not taking advantage of your library. All you have to do—if you're at all confused about tracking down the information you need—is ask the librarian.

As a matter of fact, even if you consider yourself something of a library expert, always ask your librarian for help! Make the "information" desk at the library a regular hangout. Tell the librarians what you're working on. They will know the best sources of information for your particular topic. Consult with your librarian throughout your research. You'll find information faster. And you'll get the most out of your library.

Beyond the Encyclopedia

When you were younger, you probably relied solely on the encyclopedias in your school library when you had to write a report. If you're working on a paper, yes, you may want to read encylopedias to get a general overview of your topic. But you need to turn to other sources for more detailed information. You should read books written by experts in the field you're researching. You should read magazine and newspaper articles about your subject.

And don't stop there! Pamphlets, brochures, government documents, specialized anthologies, films and videos. These are just some of the other possible sources of information you can use for paper-writing, research, enhancing your text reading and preparing for oral reports.

Where to look for materials

You should review as wide a variety of reference materials as possible.

But how do you find out whether anyone has written a magazine or newspaper article about your topic? How do you know if there are any government documents or pamphlets that might be of help? How do you locate those written-by-the-experts reference books?

You look in your library's publication indexes. These indexes list all of the articles, books and other materials that have been published and/or are available in your library.

I've listed some of the major publication indexes below. There are many, many others, so remember to ask your librarian for additional suggestions.

    1. *The Card Catalog:* This is a list of all the books in your library. (Although many libraries now store it on computer, it's still often called a card catalog because it used to be kept on index cards.) Books are indexed in three different ways: by subject, by author and by title.

2. *Newspaper Indexes:* Several large-city newspapers provide an indexed list of all articles they have published.

3. *Periodical Indexes:* To find out if any magazine articles have been published on your subject, go to a periodical index. *The Readers' Guide to Periodical Literature,* which indexes articles published in the most popular American magazines, may be one with which you're familiar.

4. *Vertical File:* Here's where you'll find pamphlets and brochures.

5. *U.S. Documents Monthly Catalog:* Useful for locating government publications.

Other resources

When you're searching for hard-to-find information, you also may want to check the following:

1. *Special Anthologies, Almanacs and Encyclopedias:* Providing more in-depth information than general encyclopedias, these are entire series devoted exclusively to specific topics.

2. *Association Directories:* An association or organization related to your topic can be one of your most valuable sources of information. Often, such organizations have a historian who can provide you with extensive literature—or, better yet, the names of experts whom you might interview! You can find their names and addresses here.

Many libraries print a list of its resources and a map of where they can be found. What if yours doesn't? That's right...you ask your librarian for help.

Your approach to research

All of us who have become familiar with the wonders of the library has probably developed our own approach to enjoying them and using them most efficiently. My own experience emphasizes what may be the obvious: Getting the right start is all important. Since I try to keep from being overwhelmed with material, I start any research working with the broadest outlines or topics (and the broadest resources) and wind my way down the ladder, getting more and more specific in topic and sources as I go.

Let's assume, for example, that you have to prepare a report on the latest attempts to combat apartheid and fit this effort into a historical perspective. Here's how you might approach the task:

1. **Go to a dictionary** and look up the term apartheid. Make certain you have a firm understanding of what this word means before you proceed any further!

2. Consult any one of the numerous leading **encyclopedias** you will find in your library—Britannica, Americana, Collier's, World Book, etc. Here you'll find an overview and historical prospective on the subject of these special racial laws. Encyclopedic entries are usually the most comprehensive and concise you will find. They cover so much territory and are so (relatively) up to date that they are an ideal "big-picture" resource.

3. With overview in hand, you can start consulting the **major indexes and directories** your library has to develop a list of more specific resources. Obviously, the entries in these major resources can then be directly consulted—specific *New York Times* issues on microfilm, periodicals at the periodicals desk, etc. And, of course, your card catalog or computer terminal will spew out listings for hundreds of other books on the general issue of apartheid or any related subject it touches (which you learned about through your skimming of the above general resources)—The African National Congress, Nelson and Winnie Mandela, Prime Minister Botha, black homelands, Archbishop Desmond Tutu, etc.

In one brief tour of your library's resources, you'll easily discover and know how to obtain more material than you would need to write a book on apartheid, let alone a report.

What if you're uncomfortable in the library? An infrequent user? Or simply find it a confusing place that's more trouble than it's worth?

As I've emphasized, developing *any* habit is just a matter of practice. The more you use the library, the more comfortable you will become using it. And, of course, the more books you will become comfortable with. In a very short time, you will have your own "personal" list of resources that you start with whenever you receive an assignment.

If you want the library to become like a second home, its every shelf a familiar friend, why not go to work there? Many libraries, smaller ones in particular, often offer opportunities for paid and volunteer work. Even if you work for free, this is an excellent way to learn the ins and outs of your library.

Many of you might not use the library as much as you should (or even would like) because it's just a confusing series of catacombs. The more comfortable you are—the more you know about the materials it contains and how to locate and use them—the more you will *want* to be there.

And the more help you will be able to obtain from this great resource that's just waiting to welcome you!

Chapter 7

HOW TO

Write Better Papers

Trust me. It's going to happen. Whether you like it or not. Sooner or later, you'll have to prepare written and/or oral reports for virtually every one of your classes. And if you're like most students, your reaction will be the same every time: "Why me? What do I do? Where do I start?"

I'm not going to pretend that reading this chapter will make you such a good writer that you can quit school and start visiting bookstores to preen in front of the window displays featuring your latest best seller.

But there is absolutely no reason to fear a paper or oral report. Once you know the simple steps to take and rules to follow to complete it satisfactorily. Once you realize that 90% of preparing a paper has *nothing* to do with writing... or even being *able* to write.

And once you're confident that preparing papers by following my suggestions will probably get you a grade or two higher than you've gotten before...even if you are the world's poorest excuse for a writer.

The Five Basic Rules

Let's start with the basic rules that need to be emblazoned on your wall:

1. *Always* follow your teacher's directions to the letter.
2. *Always* hand in your paper on time.
3. *Always* hand in a clean and clear copy of your paper.
4. *Never* allow a spelling or grammatical error in your papers.
5. *Always* keep at least one copy of every paper you write.

Follow directions

Your teacher's directions may include:

- A general subject area from which topics should be chosen—"some aspect of Roosevelt's presidency," "a 19th-century invention," "a short story by Edgar Allan Poe," etc.
- Specific requirements regarding format—typed, double-spaced, include title page, do not include title page, etc.
- Suggested length—e.g., 10-15 typewritten pages.
- Other requirements—turn in general outline before topic is approved; get verbal okay on topic before proceeding; don't include

quotes (from other works) longer than a single paragraph; and any other idiosyncrasies of your own teachers.

Whatever his or her directions, **follow them** *to the letter.* High school teachers may be somewhat forgiving, but I have known college professors who simply refused to accept a paper that was not prepared as they instructed—and gave the poor but wiser student an "F" for it (without even *reading* it).

If you are unsure of a specific requirement or if the suggested area of topics is unclear, it is *your* responsibility to talk to your teacher and clarify whatever points are confusing you.

It is also not a bad idea to choose two or three topics you'd like to write about and seek his or her preliminary approval if the assignment seems particularly vague.

Be on time

Since you've studied and memorized chapter 4, there is certainly no reason, short of catastrophic illness or life-threatening emergency, for you to *ever* be late with an assignment. Barring those, there is rarely an acceptable excuse for being late. Again, some teachers will refuse to accept a paper that is late. At best, they will do so but mark you down for your lateness, perhaps turning an "A" paper into a "B"...or worse.

Appearance counts

Teachers have to read a lot of papers and shouldn't be faulted for being human if, after hundreds of pages, they come upon your jelly-stained, pencil-written tome and get a bit discouraged. Nor should you be surprised if they give

you a lower grade than the content might merit just because the presentation is so poor.

I am not advocating "form over substance." Far from
it—the content is what the teacher is looking for, and he or
she will primarily be basing your grade on *what* you write.
But presentation is important. So follow these simple
rules:

- Never handwrite your paper.

- If you type (or have someone else type) your
  paper, use clean white bond and (preferably)
  a new carbon ribbon so that the images are
  crisp and clear.

- Unless otherwise instructed, always double
  space a typewritten paper.

- Use a simple typeface that is clear and easy-
  to-read; avoid those that are too big—stretching a five-page paper to ten—or too small
  and hard to read.

- And never use a fancy italic, modern or any
  other ornate or hard-to-read typeface for the
  entire paper.

Three! Three! Three jobs in one!

As you tackle your assignment, you actually have
three different jobs ahead of you:

1. *You must search for information.* First, you
   will dig up all the facts you can about the
   subject. You will gather statistics, historical
   data, first-person accounts and other data.
   You will read reference books, newspaper
   stories, magazine articles, scholarly jour-
   nals and other materials. You may watch a

relevant video or film, even interview a real-live expert or two.

As you do all of this, your role is like that of a *reporter*. Your job is to find out the truth. You must gather data with an unbiased eye. You can't discard or ignore information that doesn't fit in with your personal opinions or expectations.

2. **You must analyze the data.** Once you have gathered information, you must study all the data—again, from an objective viewpoint. Like a scientist evaluating the results of an experiment, you must review the evidence and decide what it means. You must draw a conclusion about your subject.

3. **You must report your findings.** Finally, you must share your new-found knowledge. You will write an in-depth report, and tell your readers what you have learned.

The Fry paper-writing system

The more complex a task or the longer you need to complete it, the more important your organization becomes. By breaking down any paper-writing project into a series of manageable steps, you'll start to feel less chaotic, hectic and scared right away.

Here are the steps that, with some minor variations along the way, are common to virtually any written report or paper:

1) Finalize your topic

2) Carry out initial library research

3) Prepare a general outline

4) Do detailed library research

5) Prepare detailed outline (from note cards)

6) Write your first draft

7) Do additional research (if necessary)

8) Write your second draft

9) Spell check and proofread

10) Have someone *else* proofread

11) Produce a final draft

12) Proofread one last time

13) Turn it in and collect your "A"

Create a work schedule

Get out your calendar. Find the date on which your paper is due. How many weeks till then? Plan to spend half of that time on research, the other half on writing.

Now, block out set periods of time during each week to work on your paper. Schedule two- or three-hour chunks of work time, rather than many short periods.

As you make up your work schedule, set deadlines for completing various steps of your paper. For example:

Week 1:	Decide on topic and "angle" of your paper.
Week 2:	Make list of references.
Weeks 3/4:	Read reference materials; take notes.
Weeks 5/6:	Do detailed outline; write first draft.
Week 7:	Edit paper; prepare bibliography.
Week 8:	Proofread paper; type final copy.

Of course, I can't tell you exactly how much time to set aside, because I don't know the specifics of your paper or your work speed. I *can* tell you that you should plan on consulting and/or taking notes from at least 10 different books, articles or other reference materials. (Your teacher or subject may demand more.) And you should plan on writing two or three drafts of your paper before you arrive at the final copy.

Refer to your work schedule often, and adjust your speed if you find yourself lagging behind.

Step 1: Choose your topic

In some cases, your teacher will assign your topic. In others, your teacher will assign a general area of study, but you will have the freedom to pick a specific topic within that general area.

But there are some pitfalls you must avoid. Let's say you need to write a 15-page paper for your American history class. And you decide your topic will be "America's Role in World War II." Can you really cover that in *15* pages? Not unless you simply rehash the high points, *à la* your third-grade history book. You could write *volumes* on the subject (many people have!) and have plenty left to say.

Instead, you need to focus on a particular, limited angle of your subject—e.g., "The Role of the Women Air Force Service Pilots in World War II."

By the same token, you must not get too narrow in your focus. Choose a subject that's too limited, and you might run out of things to say on the second page of your paper. "The Design of the Women Air Force Service Pilots' Insignia" might make an interesting one- or two-page story. It won't fill 10 or 15 pages.

Pick a topic that's too obscure, and you may find that little or no information has been written about it. In which

case, you will have to conduct your own experiments...
interview your own research subjects...and come up with
your own, original data.

Taking all of the above into consideration, do a little
brainstorming now about possible topics for your paper.
Don't stop with the first idea—come up with several different possibilities. Put this book down until you have a list
of three or four potential topics.

Step 2: Begin initial library research

Got your list? Then get thee to a library. You need to do
a little advance research. Skim your library's card-catalog
index and *Readers' Guide to Periodical Literature* or other
publication indexes. See how many books and articles
have been written about each topic on your "possibilities"
list. Next, read a short background article or encyclopedia
entry about each topic.

With any luck at all, you should be left with at least one
topic that looks like a good research subject. If two or more
topics passed your preliminary-research test, pick the one
that interests you most. You're going to spend a lot of time
learning about your subject. There's no rule that says you
can't enjoy it!

Develop a temporary thesis

Once you have chosen the topic for your paper, you
must make another important step: You must develop a
temporary thesis. (The word "thesis" is a relative of "hy-
pothesis"—and means about the same thing: the central
argument you will attempt to prove or disprove in your
paper.)

A thesis statement is a one-sentence summary of your
thesis. It sums up the main point of your paper.

Note that I said *temporary* thesis. It may not wind up being your final thesis. Because you haven't completed all your research yet, you can only come up with a "best-guess" thesis at this point.

Some teachers require that you submit your thesis statement for their approval. Even if this is not required, getting your instructor's opinion is always a good idea. Your teacher will be able to help you determine whether your thesis argument is on target.

Step 3: Create a temporary outline

Once you have developed your temporary thesis, give some thought as to how you might approach the subject in your paper. Jot down the various issues you plan to investigate. Then, come up with a brief, temporary outline of your paper, showing the order in which you might discuss those issues.

Don't worry too much about this outline—it will be brief, at best. It's simply a starting point for your research, a plan of attack. But don't skip this step, either—it will be a big help in organizing your research findings.

Step 4: Do detailed library research

We've already reviewed the library and how to take advantage of its resources. Now, let's talk about exactly how you'll keep track of all the resources and information you'll gather for your paper.

Essential ingredients: 3-by-5 index cards

To create your working bibliography, you'll need a supply of 3-by-5 index cards. You'll also use index cards when you take notes for your paper, so buy a big batch now. About 300 cards ought to suffice.

While you're stocking up on index cards, pick up one of those little envelope files designed to hold the cards. Put your name, address and phone number on the file. If you lose it, some kind stranger can return it.

Start a systematic search for any materials that might have information related to your paper. Look through the indexes we covered in Chapter 6 and any other indexes your librarian recommends.

When you find a book, article or other resource that looks promising, take out a blank note card. On the front of the card, write down the following information.

In the upper right-hand corner of the card: The library call number (Dewey decimal number or Library of Congress number), if there is one. Add any other detail that will help you locate the material on the library shelves (e.g. "Science Reading Room," "Reference Room," "Microfiche Periodicals Room").

On the main part of the card: The author's name, if given—last name first, first name, middle name/initial.

Then the title of the article, if applicable, in quotation marks.

Then the name of the book, magazine, newspaper or other publication—underlined.

Add any details you will need if you have to find the book or article again, e.g., date of publication, edition, volume number and page numbers on which the article or information appears.

In the upper left-hand corner of the card: Number it. The first card you write will be #1, the second, #2, and so on. If you happen to mess up and skip a number somewhere along the line, don't worry. It's only important that you assign a different number to each card.

At the bottom of the card: If you're going to be working in more than one library, write the name of the library.

Also write down the name of the index in which you found the resource, in case you need to refer to it again.

Do this for *each* potential source of information you find. ***And put only one resource on each card.***

Sample Bibliography Card For A Book

```
(1)                                    315.6
                            Main Reading Room

                       Jones, Karen A.
          The Life and Times of Bob Smith.
                   (see esp. pp. 43-48)



                         Card Catalog
                     Main Street Library
```

Sample Bibliography Card
For A Magazine Article

```
(2)                             Periodical Room

                      Perkins, Stan
          "The Life and Times of Bob Smith"
                    Smith Magazine
             (April 24, 1989; pp. 22-26)



                      Readers' Guide
                     University Library
```

Sample Bibliography Card
For A Newspaper Article

```
(3)                    Microfiche Room

              Black, Bill
  "Bob Smith: The New Widget Spinner"
            New York Times
  (June 16, 1976, late edition, p. A12)


          New York Times Index
            Main Street Library
```

Now hit the books

Set aside solid blocks of time for your library work. It's better to schedule a handful of extended trips to the library than 15 or 20 brief visits. When you go to the library, take your bibliography cards, a good supply of blank index cards, your preliminary outline and several pens or pencils.

Your bibliography cards are the map for your information treasure hunt. Get out a stack of five or six cards, and locate the materials listed on those cards. Set up camp at a secluded desk or table, and get to work.

How to take notes

As I said, when you write your paper, you'll get all the information you need from your notes, rather than from the original sources. Therefore, it's vital that you take careful and complete notes.

What sort of information should you put in your notes? Anything related to your subject and especially to your thesis. This includes:

1. General background information—names, dates, historical data, etc.
2. Research statistics
3. Quotes by experts
4. Definitions of technical terms

You may be used to keeping your notes in a three-ring binder or notepad. I'm going to show you a better way—recording all of your notes on index cards.

As was the case with your bibliography cards, you must follow some specific guidelines in order for this system to work. You'll want to refer to the guidelines in this chapter often during your first few note-taking sessions. After that, the system will become second nature to you.

Complete your bibliography card

Let's say that you have found a reference book that contains some information about your subject. Before you begin taking notes, get out the bibliography card for that book.

First, check that all of the information on your card is correct. Is the title exactly as printed on the book? Is the author's name spelled correctly?

Next, add any other information you will need to include in your final bibliography. The type of information you need to put on your bibliography card depends on the type of reference material and the bibliography format you are required to use.

Different authorities have put forth different bibliography rules. Be sure to ask your instructor which rules you are to follow! (For more information on exactly what you need to include, be sure to refer to **Write Papers**, one of the five books in my **HOW TO STUDY** *Program*, which includes details on bibliographic and source note formats.)

Start taking notes

Once your bibliography card is finished, set it aside. Get out some blank index cards, and start taking notes from your reference source. Follow these guidelines:

- **Write one thought, idea, quote or fact on each card.** If you encounter a very long quote or string of data, you can write on both the front and back of a card, if necessary. *But never carry over a note to a second card.*

  What if you simply *can't* fit the piece of information on one card? You're dealing with too much information at once. Break it down into two or more smaller pieces, then put each on a separate card.

- **Write in your own words.** Summarize key points about a paragraph or section. Or, restate the material in your own words. Avoid copying things word for word.

- **Put quotation marks around any material copied verbatim.** It's okay to include in your paper a sentence or paragraph written by someone else to emphasize a particular point (providing you do so on a limited basis). But you must copy such statements *exactly as written* in the original—every word, every comma, every period. You also should put each such quote within quotation marks.

Adding detail to your note cards

As you finish each note card, do the following:

- *In the upper left-hand corner of the card:* Write down the resource number of the corresponding bibliography card (in its left-hand corner). This will remind you where you got the information.

- *Below the resource number:* Write down the page(s) on which the information appeared.

- Get out your preliminary outline. Under which outline topic heading does the information on your note card seem to fit? Under your "A" heading? Under "C?" *Jot the appropriate topic letter in the upper right-hand corner of your note card.*

  If you're not sure where the information fits into your outline, put an asterisk (*) instead of a topic letter. Later, when you do a more detailed outline, you can try to fit these "miscellaneous" note cards into specific areas.

- *Next to the topic letter:* Jot down a one- or two-word "headline" that describes the information on the card.

- *When you have finished taking notes from a particular resource,* put a check mark on the bibliography card. This will let you know that you're done with that resource.

Be sure that you transfer information accurately to your note cards. Double-check names, dates and other statistics. As with your bibliography cards, it's not so important that you put each of these elements in the places

I've outlined above. You just need to be consistent. Always put the page number in the same place, in the same manner. Ditto with the resource number, the topic heading and the headline.

Sample Completed Note Card

```
┌─────────────────────────────────────────┐
│  (2)                                C     │
│  p. 22              Education—Degrees     │
│                                           │
│  Smith awarded honorary degrees in        │
│  law from both Harvard & Princeton        │
│                                           │
└─────────────────────────────────────────┘
```

Add your personal notes

Throughout your note-taking process, you may want to make some "personal" note cards. On these cards, jot down any thoughts, ideas or impressions you may have about your subject or your thesis.

Perhaps you've thought of a great introduction for your paper. Put it on a card. Or maybe you've thought of a personal experience that relates to your topic. Put it on a card.

Write each thought on a separate note card, as you have with information you've taken from other resources. And assign your note card a topic heading and mini-headline, too. In the space where you would normally put the number of the resource, put your own initials. This will tell you later that you were the source of the information or thought.

Step 5: Prepare a detailed outline

It's time to organize your data. You need to decide if your temporary thesis is still on target. You need to determine how you will organize your paper. And you need to create a detailed outline.

Sort your note cards

Once you have your final thesis, begin thinking about how you will organize your paper. This is where the note-card system really pays off. Your note cards give you a great tool for organizing your paper. Get out all of your note cards. Then:

1. Group together all of the cards that share the same outline topic letter (the letter in the right-hand corner of your note card).

2. Put those different groups in order, according to your temporary outline. (Put all of your topic "A" cards at the front of the stack of cards, followed by topic "B" cards, then topic "C" cards, etc.)

3. Within each topic group, sort the cards further. Put together all of the cards that share the same "headline" (the two-word title in the upper-right hand corner of the note card).

4. Go through your miscellaneous topic cards, the ones you marked with an asterisk. Can you fit any of them into your existing topic groups? If you can, replace the asterisk with the topic letter. If you can't, put the card at the very back of your stack of cards.

Your note cards now should be organized according to your preliminary outline. Take a few minutes to read through your note cards, beginning at the front of the stack and moving through to the back. What you actually read will be a sketchy draft of your paper. You're reading information in the order you planned to present it in your paper. Does that order still make sense? Or would another arrangement work better?

If necessary, revise your general outline according to the organizational decision you just made. However, don't change the letters that you have assigned to the topics in your outline. (If you decide to put topic B first in your new outline, keep using the letter B in front of it.) Otherwise, the topic letters on your note cards won't jibe with your outline.

Next, go through each group of cards that share the same topic letter. Rearrange them so that they, too, follow the organizational pattern you chose.

Add any miscellaneous cards. After you sort all the cards that have been assigned a specific topic heading (A, B, C, etc.), review cards that are marked with an asterisk. Try to fit them into place in your stack of cards.

Your detailed outline is done!

Flip through your note cards from front to back. See that? You've created a detailed outline without even knowing it. The topic letters on your note cards match the main topics of your outline. And those headlines on your note cards? They're the subtopics for your outline.

Simply transfer your note card headlines to paper. They appear on your outline in the same order as they appear in your stack of cards.

Some instructors require that you get their approval of your outline before going ahead with your paper. If you have to do this, find out the specific outline format you are to follow. You may need to use a specific numbering/lettering format, such as Roman numerals instead of capital letters for topic headings.)

Here's an example of a detailed outline for a paper on women pilots in World War II.

Sample Detailed Outline

The Women's Air Force Service in World War II

A. Why civilian women pilots entered the war effort

    1. Shortage of male pilots

    2. Women pilot proposal

    3. Test program begun

B. The type and number of women who participated

    1. Statistics on number of initial participants

    2. Background information about leaders of the program

    3. Participants' socio-economic background

C. Their qualifications and training

    1. Experience needed to be accepted into the program

    2. Training program

        a. ground school

        b. flight school

D. Their missions and contributions
  1. Ferrying planes
  2. Towing targets
  3. Testing repaired planes
  4. Success vs. male pilots
E. The military vs. civilian status question
  1. Reason for initial civilian status
  2. Plan to militarize
  3. Why plan was needed
  4. Why plan was not carried out
F. The disbanding of the group
  1. Additional pilots no longer needed
  2. Male pilots wanted jobs taken over by women
  3. Support for/against disbanding
G. The fight to be recognized as veterans
  1. Importance of the fight
    a. veterans' benefits for the women
    b. recognition of the group's contributions
  2. Instrumental women in the fight
  3. Debate and vote in Congress
  4. Outcome and effect of vote

Step 6: Write the first draft

Actually, you'll find this step easier than you might anticipate. That's assuming that you've done everything as instructed so far—taken good notes, organized your note cards, prepared a detailed outline, etc.

Good writing takes concentration and thought. And concentration and thought require quiet—and lots of it! You also need to have plenty of desk space, so you can spread out your note cards in front of you. Your work area should be well lit. And you should have a dictionary and thesaurus close at hand.

If possible, work on a computer, so that you can add, delete and rearrange your words easily.

Remember: At this point, your goal is to produce a rough draft—with the emphasis on *rough*. Your first draft isn't supposed to be perfect. It's *supposed* to need revision.

Your thoughts are the foundation of your paper. And you should build the foundation before you worry about the trimmings. So, for now, concentrate just on getting your thoughts on paper. Don't worry about using exactly the right word. Don't worry about getting commas in all the right places. We'll take care of all that later.

Do a note card draft

Your note cards helped you come up with a detailed outline. Now, they're going to help you plot out the actual paragraphs and even sentences of your paper.

1. Your note cards should be arranged in the same order as your detailed outline. Take out all of the note cards labeled with the letter of the first topic on your outline.

2. Out of that stack, take out all the cards marked with the same "headline" as the first subheading in your outline.

3. Look at the information on those cards. Think about how the various pieces of information might fit together in a paragraph.

4. Rearrange those cards so they fall in the order you have determined is best for the paragraph.

5. Do this for each group of cards, until you reach the end of the deck.

Now put it all on paper

Take the plunge now, and turn your note card draft into a written rough draft. Using your cards as your guide, sit down and write.

Double- or triple-space your draft, so that it will be easy to edit later on. After you are finished with a note card, put a check mark at the bottom of the card.

If you decide that you won't include information from a particular card, don't throw the card away...yet. Keep it in a separate stack. You may decide to fit in that piece of information in another part of your paper. Or you may change your mind after you read your rough draft and decide to include the information as planned after all.

Help for when you get stuck

Got writer's block already? Here are a few tricks to get you unstuck.

- Pretend you're writing a letter to a good friend, and tell him or her everything you have learned about your subject and why you believe your thesis is correct.

- Use everyday language. Too many people get so hung up on using fancy words and phrases that they forget that their goal is communication. Simpler is better. Drop the "dollar" words and settle for the twenty-five centers.

- Type *some*thing. Once you have written that first sentence—even if it's a really *bad* first sentence—your brain will start to generate spontaneous ideas.
- Don't edit yourself! As you write your rough draft, don't keep beating yourself up with negative. Remember, your goal is a *rough* draft.
- Keep moving. If you get hung up in a particular section, don't sit there stewing over it for hours...or even very many minutes. Just write a quick note about what you plan to cover in that section, and go on.
- If you can't get even that much out, skip the section altogether and come back to it later. The point is, do whatever you have to do to keep moving forward. Force yourself to make it all the way through your paper, with as few stops as possible.

Document your sources

To avoid plagiarism, you must document the source when you put any of the following in your paper:

- Quotations taken from a published source
- Someone else's theories or ideas
- Someone else's sentences, phrases or special expressions
- Facts, figures and research data compiled by someone else
- Graphs, pictures and charts designed by someone else

There are some exceptions. You don't need to document the source of a fact, theory or expression that is common knowledge. And you don't need a source note when you use a phrase or expression for which there is no known author.

Footnotes

For many years, the preferred way to credit sources was the footnote. Two other forms of documentation, endnotes and parenthetical notes, are popular now as well.

A footnote is a source note that appears at the bottom of a page of text. You put a raised (superscript) number at the end of the statement or fact you need to document., which tells your readers to look at the bottom of the page for a note about the source of the data.

What goes in a footnote? The same information that's in the bibliography listing. *And* the exact page number the information appears on.

In front of that source note, you put the same superscript number as you put next to the statement or fact in your text.

There is no limit to the number of footnotes you may have in your paper. Number each footnote consecutively, starting with the number 1. For every footnote "flag" in your paper, be sure there is a corresponding source note at the bottom of the page.

Different strokes

Like bibliography listings, different authorities cite different rules for setting up footnotes. Ask your teacher whose rules you are to follow. If your teacher doesn't have a preference, you might as well use the Modern Language

Association of America (MLA) rules, which I do. Also, be sure to refer to *Write Papers* for a more in-depth examination of source documentation. Using the hypothetical paper below, I've included some sample footnotes, based on MLA guidelines, for a book, a magazine article and a newspaper article.

> Bob Smith was a leader in the history of Smiths in America. He earned $1 milion by the time he was 18.[1] He was awarded honorary degrees in law from Harvard and Princeton.[2] At the age of 35, he invented the first successful widget-spinning gadget,[3] which gave manufacturers a new way to produce widgets.
>
> More than a savvy businessman and accomplished scholar, Smith was a devoted family man. A close friend and neighbor, Bill Jones, once said of Smith: "I never met a man who spent so much time attending to the needs of his wife and children."[4]

[1] Karen A. Jones, The Life and Times of Bob Smith (New York: Smith Press, 1989) 24.

[2] Stan Perkins, "The Life and Times of Bob Smith," Smith Magazine 24 Apr. 1989: 22.

[3] Bill Black, "Bob Smith: The New Widget Spinner," New York Times 16 June 1976, late ed.: A12.

[4] Jones 38.

Step 7: Do additional research

Did you discover any gaps in your research as you put together your first draft? Raise some questions that you need additional information to answer? Then now's the time to head for the library for one last crack at the books.

Step 8: Write the second draft

The goal for this phase is to edit for meaning: to improve the flow of your paper, organize your thoughts better, clarify confusing points and strengthen any weak arguments.

At this stage, you will focus on all of those problem areas you found. Add new data or information, if need be. Play with sentences, paragraphs and even entire sections. If you're working with a computer, this is fairly easy to do. You can flip words, cut and add sentences, or rearrange whole pages with a few keystrokes.

If you're working with a typewriter or pencil and paper, you can do the same thing, but with scissors and tape. Just cut up the pages of your rough draft, and tape them together in their new order.

After you've fixed major problem areas, take an even closer look at your sentences and paragraphs. Try to make them smoother, tighter, easier to understand.

- Is there too much fat? Seize every opportunity to say it in fewer words.

- Are there places where phrasing or construction is awkward? Rearrange your words so they "flow" better.

- Did you use descriptive, colorful words? Did you simply tell your reader, "The last days of the war were hard?" Or did you inform them that "the war dragged on, for days...weeks...months, as weary soldiers slogged from battle to bloody battle."

  Consult your thesaurus for synonyms that might do a better job than the words you originally chose. But don't get carried away and use words so obscure that the

average reader wouldn't know their meaning. Or that fall on the reader's ear with a
"we - don't - really - belong - here - but - we -
are - impressive - aren't - we?" clamor.

- Have you overused particular words? Constantly relying on the same verb or adjective
makes your writing boring. Again, check
your thesaurus for other possibilities.

- How do the words *sound?* When you read
your paper aloud, does it flow like a wonder-
fully rhythmic piece of music? Or just thud
along like a dull dirge? Vary the length of
your sentences and paragraphs to make
your writing more exciting.

Again, mark corrections on your draft with a colored
pen or pencil. No need to retype your paper yet — unless it's
gotten so marked up that it's hard to read.

When you finish editing for content and meaning,
print or type out a clean copy of your paper.

Step 9: Check spelling and proofread

All right, here's the part that almost nobody enjoys:
It's time to rid your paper of mistakes in grammar and
spelling.

I know that I've told you your thoughts are the most
important element of your paper. It's true. But it's also
true that glaring mistakes in grammar and spelling will
lead your teacher to believe that you are either careless or
downright ignorant. Neither of which will bode well for
your final grade.

So, get out your dictionary and a reference book on
English usage and grammar. Scour your paper, sentence

by sentence, marking corrections with your colored pen or pencil. Look for:

- *Misspelled words.* Check every word. Ask yourself, "If I had to bet $100 that I spelled that word correctly, would I take the bet?" No? Then you better look it up in the dictionary.
- *Incorrect punctuation.* Review the rules for placement of commas, quotation marks, periods, etc. Make sure that you follow those rules throughout your paper.
- *Incorrect sentence structure.* Look for dangling participles, split infinitives, sentences that end in prepositions and other no-no's. Again, review the rules about such matters in your reference book.

Step 10: Have someone *else* proofread

Retype your paper, making all those corrections you marked during the last step. Format the paper according to the teacher's instructions. Incorporate your final footnotes and bibliography.

Give your paper a title, if you haven't already done so. Your title should be as short and sweet as possible, but tell readers what they can expect to learn from your paper.

Find someone who is a good proofreader—a parent, relative, friend—and ask him or her to proofread your paper before you put together the final draft.

Steps 11 and 12: The final draft

Incorporate any changes or errors your proofreader may have caught. Type the final draft.

Proof it again—very carefully.

When everything's absolutely perfect, head right for the copy shop. Pay the buck or two it costs to make a copy of your paper. After all your hard work, you want to be sure you have a backup copy in case you lose or damage your original.

Last step? Put your paper in a new manuscript binder or folder. Then, turn it in—on time, of course!

Oral reports

There are some key differences between writing a report and presenting it orally, especially if you don't want to make the mistake of just reading your report in front of the class.

Good notes are your lifeline when you stand up to say what's on your mind. They should act as cues to remind you where your talk should go next, and they should make you feel secure that you can get through the ordeal.

However, notes can also be a crutch that guarantees not success, but audience boredom. You've probably seen any number of people get up in front of an audience and just read some papers they have in front of them.

Is there any *better* cure for insomnia?

As you gather information for your report, making notes on index cards as you did for your term paper, keep this in mind: In order for you to be effective, you must use some different techniques when you *tell* your story rather than *write* it. Here are a few:

- ***Don't make your topic too broad.*** This advice, offered for preparing written reports as well, is even more important when preparing a talk. Try giving an effective speech on "Drugs," "Hamlet" or

"Capital Punishment"...in 15 minutes, frequently the amount of time assigned for oral reports. These topics are more suited to a series of books!

"How Shakespeare portrays Hamlet As The Mad Prince" or "Why Drugs Should (or Shouldn't) Be Legalized" or "Why Capital Punishment Is No Deterrent" are more manageable. Narrowing the scope of your talk will help you research and organize it more effectively.

- *Don't overuse statistics.* While they're very important for lending credibility to your position, too many will only weigh down your speech and bore your audience—as anyone who sat through one of the last presidential debates can tell you.

- *Anecdotes add color and life to your talk.* But use them sparingly, because they can slow down your speech. Get to the punch-line before the yawns start.

- *Be careful with quotes.* Unlike a term paper, a speech allows you to establish yourself as an authority with less fear of being accused of plagiarism. So you can present a lot more facts without attribution. (But you'd better have the sources in case you're asked about your facts.) You can use quotes, though, when they contain distinctive language or elicit an emotion. Be sure to attribute the source.

I've found that trying to shuffle a bunch of papers in front of a class is difficult and that note cards that fit in the palm of your hand are a lot easier to use. But only if the notes on them are very short and to the point, to act as "triggers" rather than verbatim cue cards—hanging on to 300 note cards is as difficult as a sheaf of papers.

Remember: You'll actually be holding these cards in your sweaty palms and speaking from them, so write *notes,* not whole sentences. The shorter the notes—and the more often you practice your report so each note triggers the right information—the more effective your report will be. (And the less you will have to look at them, making eye contact with your class and teacher easier.)

As far as ways to make your oral reports more effective, we've already talked about some in chapter 5, but here are a few more:

- Pick out one person to talk to—preferably a friend, but an animated and/or interested person will do—and direct your talk to them.

- Practice, *practice,* **practice** your presentation. Nerves are often because of a lack of confidence. The more confident you are that you know your material, the less nervous you will be. And the better and more spontaneous your presentation will be.

- If you are like me and suffer from the involuntary "shakes" at the mere thought of standing in front of a roomful of people, make sure you can use a lectern, desk or something to cling to.

- Take a deep breath before you go to the front of the class. And don't worry about pausing, even taking another deep breath or two, if you lose your place or find your confidence slipping away.

- If every trick in the world still doesn't steady you down, consider taking a public speaking course (Dale Carnegie, *et al),* joining the Toastmasters Club, or seeking out similar extracurricular help.

I've begun to think of my notes for speeches as the purest form of the note-taking craft we've described in this book. You are distilling ideas down to a phrase, a word, a number, perhaps a symbol that will help you remember under pressure.

Often, the very *process* of taking notes is enough, in itself, to ensure that a fact, an impression or a formula will last in your memory for a long time. Note-taking is stripping data down to their essence.

Chapter 8

HOW TO

Study

For

Tests

Quizzes. Midterms. Finals.

PSAT. ACT. SAT.

GMAT. GRE. LSAT.

Civil Service exams. Aptitude tests. Employment tests.

Throughout your educational life—and, more than likely, the rest of your life as well—testing will be an inevitable if sometimes frightening and distressing reality. So the sooner you learn the techniques of preparing for, taking and mastering tests, the better off you'll be.

Testing is employed for two primary reasons. The first is to gauge your mastery of a particular subject or material. It thus helps establish the minimum standards of achievement you must attain to move up to the next rung of the ladder—the next grade, next course (acceptance to

many college courses is based on your successfully passing another course first), next pay scale, next job level.

Its second function is to determine the relative standing of one person to another. This has the desired effect of
reducing the number of applicants for a single college slot
or limiting a final job interview to those best qualified.
And, of course, of giving your teacher a "curve" on which
to grade you and your classmates.

What do they want to know?

Before you can decide how to study for a particular test,
it's imperative that you know exactly what you're being
tested *on*. Preparing for a weekly quiz is far different than
preparing for a final exam. And the biggest final of your
life is child's play compared to "monster tests" like the oral
exams I faced before they allowed me to graduate college—which covered everything I was supposed to have
learned in four years of attendance!

Studying for a standardized test like the SAT, ACT or
GRE is also completely different—you can't pull out your
textbook and, knowing what chapters are being included,
just "bone up."

The structure of the test is also of paramount importance, not necessarily in terms of how you study, but how
you tackle the test once you get your test book.

What are you afraid of?

Tests are scary creatures. So before I start meting out
test-taking techniques, let's tackle one of the key problems
many of you will face—test anxiety, that all-too-common
reaction to tests characterized by sweaty palms, a blank
mind and the insane urge to flee to Pago Pago on the next
available cargo ship.

Take heart—very few people look forward to a test; more of you are afraid of tests than you'd think. But that doesn't mean you *have* to fear them.

Since we all recognize the competitive nature of tests, being in the right frame of mind when taking them is important. Some of us rise to the occasion when facing such a challenge. Others are thrown off balance by the pressure. Both reactions probably have little to do with one's level of knowledge, relative intelligence or amount of preparation. The smartest kids in your class may be the ones most afraid of tests.

Generally speaking, the best way to avoid the pitfalls of the extraordinary pressures of a testing situation is to place yourself in that environment as often as possible. Yep. Practice helps.

But there are some other, surprisingly simple steps you can take to give yourself an edge by being less *on* edge.

Handling anxiety

Few people enter a testing site cool, calm and ready for action. Most of us have various butterflies gamboling in our stomachs, sweat glands operating in overdrive and a sincere desire to be somewhere else...*anywhere* else.

Even if you're just entering high school, you have a few years of tests under your belt and should have some idea of how well or poorly you react to a testing situation. If the answer is "not well," start trying some of the following options until you find the one(s) that work for you.

"I know I can, I know I can"

The more pressure you put on yourself—the larger you allow a test (and, of course, your hoped-for good scores) to loom in your own mind—the less you are helping yourself.

And, of course, the bigger the test really *is,* the more likely you are to keep reminding yourself of its importance.

No matter how important a test really may be to your career—and, let's face it, your scores on some *can* have a major effect on where you go to college, whether you go on to graduate school, whether you get the job you want—it is just as important to *de*-emphasize that test's importance in your mind. This should have no effect on your preparation—you should still study as if your life depended on a superior score. It might!

Keeping the whole experience in perspective might also help: Twenty years from now, nobody will remember, or care, what you scored on *any* test—no matter how life-threatening or life-determining you feel that test is right now.

And don't underestimate that old standby, positive thinking: Thoughts *can* become self-fulfilling prophecies. Tell yourself often enough "be careful, you'll fall over that step," and you probably will. Tell yourself often enough "I'm going to fail this test" and you just might. Likewise, keep convincing yourself that you are as prepared as anyone and are going to "ace" the sucker, and you are already ahead of the game.

A little traveling music, Sammy

You've already found that scheduling breaks during your study routine makes it easier for you to focus on your books and complete your assignments faster and with more concentration. Scheduling breaks during tests has the same effect.

During a one-hour test, you may not have time to go out for a stroll. But during a two- or three-hour final, a major test like the SAT, etc., there's no reason you should not schedule one, two or even more breaks on a periodic basis—whenever you feel you need them most. Such time-outs can consist of a bathroom stop, a quick walk up and down the hall, or just a minute of relaxation in your seat before you continue the test.

No matter what the time limits or pressures, don't feel you cannot afford such a brief respite. You may need it *most* when you're convinced you can *least* afford it.

I'm relaxing as fast as I can!

If your mind is a jumble of facts and figures, names and dates, you may find it difficult to zero in on the specific details you need to recall, even if you know all the material backward and forward. The adrenaline rushing through your system may just make "instant retrieval" impossible.

The simplest relaxation technique is deep breathing. Just lean back in your chair, relax your muscles and take three very deep breaths (count to 10 while you hold each one). For many of you, that's the only relaxing technique you'll ever need.

There are a variety of meditation techniques that may also work for you. Each is based on a similar principle—focusing your mind on one thing to the exclusion of everything else. While you're concentrating on the object of your meditation (even if the object is nothing, a non-sense word or a spot on the wall), your mind can't be thinking about anything else, which allows it to slow down a bit.

The next time you can't focus, try sitting back, taking three deep breaths and concentrating for a minute or two on the word "Mu." When you're done, you should be in a far more relaxed state and ready to tackle any test.

If you feel you need such help, consider learning some sort of meditation technique, whether Silva mind control, transcendental meditation, or even self-hypnosis.

Ah, hypnosis. Another alternative. While I question its effectiveness as a study method—I'm not sure if learning self-hypnosis can help you read faster, remember more, etc.—it can be an excellent relaxation technique, as it is really just a form of meditation.

Whatever such technique you feel you need to use, remember an important fact: The more you believe in the technique, the more it will work. Just like your belief that you're going to "ace" that test!

Some rites of preparation are pertinent to any test, from a weekly quiz to the SAT and everything in between:

Plan ahead

I'll admit it. When I was a student, even in college, my attention span tended to be bounded by the weekends. Tell me in October that there would be a big test the first week of December and I'd remember, probably, around November 31.

Of such habits are cramming, crib sheets and failing marks made.

The key to avoiding all of these unpleasantries is review. But *regular, periodic review.* The more often you review, the less often you will have to pull all-nighters the week of the test. You already will have stayed on top of the material, written down and asked questions that arose from your reviews and gone over class and textbook notes to make sure you understand everything. Your last-minute review will be relatively leisurely and organized, not feverish and harried.

In Chapter 4, I included a review schedule on our Project Board (see pp. 76 and 77). My suggestion is to set up the simplest review schedule possible, but one you will stick to. For example, you might simply review one subject a week until you have reviewed the previous work for each subject. Then start over again. Sunday mornings might be set aside for this process. Or a weeknight that you normally have free.

Alternatively, you can review the previous week's work in *all* subjects *every* week. Some of you may prefer this method; I personally find it a little unwieldy, preferring to concentrate on just one subject and being able to work as long as necessary without worrying about having to "move on."

Later in this chapter I will be talking about the possibility of forming a study group, which might make the review process even easier.

Get me to the church

Doing poorly on a test is discouraging. Doing poorly on a test you felt ready for is depressing. Missing the test entirely is devastating.

It's imperative that you know when and where all tests are scheduled and allow ample time to get to them.

If you're still in high school, getting to a particular test shouldn't be too hard—it will probably be held during your regular class period and in your normal classroom.

But in college, tests may be scheduled at hours different than the normal class period...and at an entirely different site.

Likewise, major out-of-school tests like the SAT may not even be held at your school. In such cases, make sure you allow enough time to drive to, or be driven to, wherever you have to be—especially if no one is quite sure how to get there!

As soon as you know the time and location of any major test—midterm, final, SAT, etc.—enter it on your weekly calendar. Whether in high school, college or grad school, most schools set aside a week, two or even more for final exams. This exam period is usually clearly marked in your college handbook, announced in class (usually on the first day), printed on your class syllabus, etc.

Optional assignments

Sometimes, in addition to your regular reading and assignments, the teacher will assign "optional" reading at the beginning of a course. These books, articles, etc. may never be discussed in any class—but material from them may well be included on a test, especially a final exam. If you have neglected to add this supplementary reading to your regular weekly assignments calendar, but wish to read it before the test, make sure you allow enough time to buy or find these books. A lot of other students may have also left such reading to the last minute, and you may be unable to find the material you need if you wait too long.

Pens, pencils...a candy bar

Lastly, bring whatever materials you need to the test, from pens and pencils to calculators. I also recommend—especially for a long test like the SAT—that you bring along a candy bar, lifesavers, Granola bar or some other "quick energy" snack to help buck you up when you need to give yourself a figurative "slap in the face."

Although many testing booklets will include room for notes, it may not be sufficient for your purposes. If you are asked to write three, five or even more essay questions, you will want a lot of scratch paper to outline and organize your thoughts before you put pen to paper. Likewise, a particularly complex math test may quickly use up every margin on the test. So bring along a separate writing tablet or even a stack of scrap paper. There are few situations in which their use won't be allowed.

If you didn't listen before...

Review, *review,* **review.** If you don't follow my advice for periodic review, you must be sure, especially for midterms and finals, to set aside the time to do the review and studying you need in the week or two before the test.

The more material you need to review, the more important it is to clear your schedule. A four-, five- or six-course load covering 20, 40 or more books, lectures and discussions, papers and projects, easily generates hundreds of pages of notes. Reviewing them, understanding them, studying them will require your full-time effort for a week, even two. So make sure all other end-of-term work, especially major projects like papers, are out of the way.

Whether you need to schedule a solid two weeks for a complete review or just two or three days because you have already reviewed most of your course work on a regular basis, make sure you schedule the time you've allocated on your weekly calendar, allowing more time for the subjects in which you are weakest, of course.

Test yourself

Yes, there are teachers who test you on the most mundane details from every book assigned, requiring you to review every book, every note, every scribble.

I don't think most teachers work that way.

The areas on which your teacher seems to place his or her emphasis—based on time spent in class, questions asked on quizzes, midterms, etc.—should be the same areas *you* concentrate on for a major test. (Which is why you should try to save copies of every test you are given. They are excellent study aids!)

In general, take the time to eliminate from consideration, with the possible exception of a cursory review, material you are convinced is not important enough to be included on an upcoming test. This will automatically give you more time to concentrate on those areas you are sure *will* be included on the test.

Just as you have made it a habit to write down questions as you study your texts, why not try to construct your own tests? And remember: The harder you make them, the better prepared and more confident you will be walking into the test.

Study groups: What are friends for?

Surprisingly enough, I was 35 and a devoted watcher of the television show *The Paper Chase* before I was introduced to the concept of a study group. Now this series was supposed to be about a Law School that seemed just this side of hell, so sharing the load with other students wasn't just a good idea, it was virtually mandatory for survival. If I had thought of the idea myself, even while I was in high school, I would have probably started one.

The idea is simple: Find a small group of like-minded students—four to six seems to be an optimal number—and share notes, question each other, prepare for tests together. To be effective, obviously, the students you pick to be in your group should share all, or at least most, of your classes.

Search out students who are smarter than you, but not *too* much smarter. If they are on a level far beyond your own, you'll soon be left in the dust and be more discouraged than ever. On the other hand, if you choose students who are too far beneath your level, you may enjoy being the "Brain" of the bunch but miss the point of the group—the challenge of other minds to spur you on.

Study groups can be organized in a variety of ways. Each member could be assigned primary responsibility for a single class, including preparing detailed notes from lectures and discussion groups. If supplementary reading is recommended but not required, that person could be responsible for doing all such reading and preparing detailed summaries.

(The extra work you will thus have to do in one class will be offset by the extra work others will be doing for you.)

Alternatively, everybody can be responsible for his or her own notes, but the group could act as an *ad hoc* discussion group, refining your understanding of key points, working on problems together, questioning each other, practicing for tests, etc.

Even if you find only one or two other students willing to work with you, such cooperation will be invaluable, especially in preparing for major exams.

420 questions!?

Is it wrong to ask the teacher what kind of test to expect?

Absolutely not.

Will he or she always tell you?

Absolutely not.

But it is also not wrong to research that teacher's tests from previous years—students a year or two ahead of you can sometimes be of invaluable help in this effort.

Why? Because, like most of us, teachers are creatures of habit. While you certainly shouldn't expect to find questions that will be duplicated, you can glean a few key things from previous tests, like the format the teacher seems to prefer and the areas that seem to be stressed.

Don't take any of this as a "given," however: Even creatures of the most set habits have been known to turn over a new leaf now and then.

The day of the test

If the test is not simply during a regular class period, make sure to arrive at the test site early. Based on your preferences (from Chapter 2), sit where you like.

Be careful, however. There may be some variations here you have to take into account. In a test where there are 200 or 300 people in a room, there is a distinct advantage to sitting near the front: You can hear instructions and the answers to questions better. And you generally get the test first.

Know the ground rules

Will you be penalized for guessing? The teacher, for example, may inform you that he will add two points for every correct answer but *subtract* one point for every incorrect one. This will certainly affect whether you guess or skip the question—or, at the very least, how many potential answers you feel you need to eliminate before the odds of guessing are in your favor.

Are the questions or sections weighted? Some tests may have two, three or more sections, some of which count for very little—10 or 20 percent of your final score—while one, usually a major essay, may be more heavily weighted—50 percent or more of your grade. This should drastically alter the time you spend on each section.

Answer every fourth question

Read and understand the directions. As I stressed in Chapter 7, you could seemingly do everything *right*, but not follow your teacher's explicit directions, in which case everything's *wrong*.

If you're supposed to check off *every* correct answer to each question in a multiple choice test—and you're assuming only *one* answer to each question is correct—you're going to miss a lot of answers!

If you're to pick one essay question out of three, or two out of five, that's a lot different than trying to answer every one. You won't do it. And even if you do, the teacher will probably only grade the first two. Because you needed to allocate enough time to do the other three, it's highly doubtful your first two answers will be so detailed and perfect that they will be able to stand alone.

And be aware of time. Again, if questions or sections are weighted, you will want to make sure you allow extra time for those that count the most. Better to do a superior job on the two sections that count for 90 percent of the score and whip through the 10-percent section as the teacher is collecting booklets.

I know students who, before they write a single answer, look through the entire test and break it down into time segments—allocating 20 minutes for section one, 40 for section two, etc. Even on multiple choice tests, they count the total number of questions, divide by the time allotted and set "goals" on what time they should reach question 10, question 25, 50, etc.

I never did it. But I think it's a great idea—if it turns out to be a workable organizational tool for you and not just one more layer of pressure.

Test-taking strategies

Presuming you know the answers to the various questions raised above, what techniques can you use to better your test scores?

There are three ways to attack a test:

1. Start at the first question and keep going, question by question, until you reach the end, never leaving a question until you have either answered it fully or, if it's a multiple choice test, made an educated guess.

2. Answer every easy question—the ones you know the answers to without any thinking at all or those requiring the simplest calculations—first, then go back and do the harder ones.

3. Answer the hardest questions first, then go back and do the easy ones.

None of these three options is inherently right or wrong. Each may work for different individuals. (And I'm assuming that these three approaches are all in the context of the test format. Weighted sections may well affect your strategy.)

The first approach is, in one sense, the quickest, in that no time is wasted reading through the whole test trying to pick out either the easiest or hardest questions. Presuming that you do not allow yourself to get stumped by a single question so that you spend an inordinate amount of time on it, it is probably the method most of you should employ (and already do).

Remember, though, to leave questions that confuse you from the outset to the end and allocate enough time to both go back to those you haven't answered and check *all* your answers thoroughly.

The second approach ensures that you will maximize your right answers—you're putting those you are certain of down first.

It may also, presuming that you knock off these easy ones relatively fast, give you the most time to work on those that you find particularly vexing.

The last approach is actually the one I use.

In fact, I make it a point to do the very hardest question first, then work my way "down" the difficulty ladder.

It may sound like a strange strategy to you, so let me explain the psychology.

First of all, I figure if time pressure starts getting to me at the end of the test, I would rather be in a position to answer the easiest questions—and a lot of them—in the limited time left than ones I really have to think about. After all, by the end of the test, my mind won't be working as well as at the beginning!

And that's a major benefit of the third approach: When I am most "up," most awake, most alert, I am tackling those questions that require the most analysis, thinking, interpretation, etc. When I am most tired—near the end— I am answering the questions that are virtually "gim-mes."

At the same time, I am also giving myself a real shot of confidence. As soon as I finish the first hard question, I already feel better. When I finish all of the hard ones, everything is downhill.

It is not the approach for everybody, but it may be for you.

I would always, however, try to ensure adequate time to at least put down an answer for every question. Better to get one question wrong and complete three other answers than get one right and leave three blank.

And don't fall into the "answer daze," that blank stare some students get when they just can't think of an answer—for 10 minutes.

Do *some*thing.

Better to move on and get that one question wrong than waste invaluable time doing nothing.

Discriminate and eliminate

There is usually nothing wrong with guessing, unless, of course, you know wrong answers will be penalized. Even then, as I've pointed out, guessing is not necessarily wrong. The question is how *much* to guess.

If there is no penalty for wrong answers, you should *never* leave an answer blank. But you should also do everything you can to increase your odds of getting it right. If every multiple-choice question gives you four possible answers, you have a 25-percent chance of being right (and, of course, a 75-percent chance of being wrong) each time you have to guess.

But if you can eliminate a single answer—one you are reasonably certain cannot be right—your chances of being correct are 33 percent.

And, of course, if you can get down to a choice between two answers, it's just like flipping a coin: 50-50. In the long run, you will guess as many right as wrong.

Even if there is a penalty for guessing, I would probably pick one answer if I had managed to increase my chances of getting the right one to 50-50.

I could write a book

Approach essay questions the same way you would a paper. While you can't check your textbook or go to the library to do research, the facts, ideas, comparisons, etc. you need are in your own cerebral library—your mind.

> *Step One:* On a blank sheet of paper, write down all the facts, ideas, concepts, etc. you feel should be included in your answer.
>
> *Step Two:* Organize them in the order in which they should appear. You don't have to

rewrite your notes into a detailed outline—
why not just number each note according to
where you want to place it?

Step Three: Compose your first paragraph,
working on it just as long and as hard as I
suggested you do on your papers. It should
summarize and introduce the key points you
will make in your essay. *This is where superior essay answers are made or broken.*

Step Four: Write your essay.

Step Five: Reread your essay and, if necessary, add points left out, correct spelling,
grammar, etc.

If there is a particular fact you know is important and
should be included but you just don't remember it, guess if
you can. Otherwise, just leave it out and do the best you
can. If the rest of your essay is well-thought-out and
organized and clearly communicates all the other points
that should be included, I doubt most teachers will mark
you down too severely for such an omission.

Remember: Few teachers will be impressed by length.
A well-organized, well-constructed, specific answer to
their question will always get you a better grade than
"shotgunning"—writing down everything you know in the
faint hope that you will actually hit something.

If you don't have the faintest clue what the question
means, ask. If you still don't have any idea of the answer—and I mean *zilch*—leave it blank. Writing down
everything you think you know about the supposed subject
in the hopes that one or two things will actually have
something to do with the question is, in my mind, a waste
of everyone's time. Better to allocate the time you would
waste to other parts of the test and do a better job on those.

First out could be first failed

Leave time at the end of every test to recheck your answers.

And speaking of time, don't make a habit of leaving tests early. There is little to be gained from supposedly "impressing" the teacher and other students with how smart you (think you) are by being first to finish. Take the time to make sure you've done your best. If you are completely satisfied with your answers to all questions, it's fine to leave, even if you are first. But in general, slowing down will help you avoid careless mistakes.

Speed kills.

Likewise, don't worry about what everybody else is doing. Even if you're the last person left, who cares? Everybody else could have failed, no matter how early and confidently they strode from the room! So take all the time you need and do the best you can.

Open-book tests

Answer the questions you don't need the book for first, including those where you're fairly sure and know where to check the answers in your book. Star these latter ones.

Then use the book. Check your starred answers first and erase the stars once you have checked. Then work on those questions on which you must rely fully on the book.

Standardized tests

The various standardized tests used in college and graduate school admissions—SAT, ACT, LSAT, GRE, etc.—require their own pointers. These, like my oral exams at the end of four years of college, are not specific to any course or even one grade. Rather, they are attempting to assess your ability to apply mathematical concepts, read and understand various passages and demonstrate word skills. (And, starting in 1992, will include an essay.)

Despite their ephemeral nature, you *can* study for them by practicing. There are a variety of companies specializing in preparing students for each of these tests—your school might even sponsor its own course. And any bookstore will probably have shelves of preparation guides.

Given their importance, I would recommend investing the time and money in any such reputable course—Stanley Kaplan, Princeton Review, BAR/BRI, etc.—or, at the very least, buying one of the major preparation books.

Because these are, indeed, *standard*ized tests, learning and utilizing specific techniques pertinent to them and practicing on tests given previously can significantly increase your scores, if only because you will feel less anxious and have a better idea of what's in store for you.

If you are an avid reader and understand what you read, do well in school in most subjects, but especially English and Math, and "test well," you may not feel you need such help. That's okay, too. But do note that many of the questions on these tests are word-related—"SWAN is to DUCK as YOGURT is to __"—testing both your basic vocabulary and your specific understanding of synonyms (words with similar meanings) and antonyms (words with opposite meanings).

So if you don't decide to take one of the review courses, you might still consider getting a good vocabulary book—*Increase Your Word Power in 30 Days* or something similar—as a study aid for such tests.

There are students who achieve exceptional test scores on their SATs and go on to compile barely adequate college records. These people are said to "test well:" The testing environment doesn't throw them and they have sufficient prior experience to have a decided edge on the rest of the competition. Others "choke" during such tests but wind up at the top of the career pyramid.

So such testing must be kept in perspective. Though one method of predicting success, such tests are not, by any means, perfect oracles. Nor are their conclusions inalienable. Many people have succeeded in life without ever doing particularly well on achievement tests.

Remember: Testing is a skill that can, to a great extent, be learned. Since it is already a part of your life and always will be, you'd be wise to take the time *now* to master the fundamentals of smart test taking. Just reading this chapter has probably helped immensely, even if all it did for you was remove some of the mystery from the testing process.

Index

How To Study